ANDREW AND MURIEL'S
HEALTHY VEGGIES MADE DELICIOUS

"Cruciferous, Leafy Greens and More"

MURIEL ANGOT

WITH ANDREW LESSMAN

PHOTOGRAPHY: LINDSEY ELTINGE
COVER PHOTOGRAPHY: JEFF STROHECKER
ASSISTANT/STYLIST: LOETTA EARNEST
ASSISTANT: KYLE KLEIN

Published by the Andrew Lessman Foundation
430 Parkson Road, Henderson, NV 89011

Printed in the United States of America.

First Printing, November 2012

ISBN 978-0-578-11531-3

Dedicated to the healthy soul in each of us…
who longs to eat well and live well.

Because you've asked...
some pictures of Lincoln.

ABOUT THE AUTHOR

Muriel Angot was born and raised in the world's center of fine cuisine – Paris, France; however, it would take Muriel a couple of decades to rediscover her Parisian culinary roots, since she initially followed in her parents' footsteps studying Fine Art at the Sorbonne University in Paris. After college, Muriel's innate curiosity and desire to explore the world saw her leave France, spending time in Australia, Fiji, New Zealand and South America, until she fell in love with the United States where she established a beauty and wellness business in Aspen, Colorado. It wasn't until Muriel chose to attend cooking school that her true passion captured her and since that time, has never let go.

Like many French families, all the members of Muriel's family take pride in their abilities in the kitchen. But it was Muriel's paternal grandmother, Simone, who was to have the greatest influence, since she was the chef and owner of a restaurant in Picardie, France – a small city in the countryside just outside Paris. Some of Muriel's fondest childhood memories are of helping her grandmother create all the classic French dishes that were served at her restaurant. The special moments she shared with her grandmother in the culturally rich environment of an authentic French kitchen were to shape the rest of Muriel's life.

When Muriel moved from Colorado to California, the move presented an opportunity for a career change and with great trepidation she decided to take the plunge. Despite hearing how challenging and difficult it would be, Muriel followed her dream and attended Le Cordon Bleu cooking school in Paris – the same school attended by Julia Child. Ultimately, she graduated #1 in her class and now considers herself blessed to combine her two greatest passions – cooking and wellness.

FOREWORD
from *Andrew Lessman*

A good place to start is with my favorite quote about vegetables:

You can live without them, but not nearly as well, nor as long.

We all know that vegetables are the healthiest part of our diet. There is nothing quite like them. *Plus, they are also the lowest in calories!* The science has been clear for decades, but given my traditional upbringing and my history with vegetables, I never expected to participate in a cookbook about "vegetables I love to eat." I suppose a little background will make that easier to understand, but anyone who knew me during the first thirty years of my life would never imagine me contributing to a cookbook on veggies – unless you consider meat, milk, eggs, ice cream, potatoes, pasta, bread or rice to be vegetables!

Given my focus on athletics, I spent the first few decades of my life constantly hungry and perpetually eating. That was why I was often referred to as the "human garbage disposal." Unfortunately, this garbage disposal did not accept vegetables. In fact, for the first thirty years of my life, eating vegetables was always a chore. My youthful diet included a gallon of whole milk daily (of course with cookies) and several eggs, along with sandwiches, lots of meat (rarely fish), potatoes, pizza, pasta and of course, my daily half gallon of ice cream. It frightens me today to write that, but I was a young athlete struggling to gain weight, so my goal was not health, but how many calories I could consume. In short, I was not making great food decisions, but then as children, we inherit the traditional eating habits of our families and as an athlete, my only goal was weight-gain. Sadly, old habits die hard, and it is impossible to change our old habits unless we learn healthier ones.

Without going too far afield, a funny story from my childhood sums up my rocky relationship with vegetables. As children, neither my sister nor I ate much in the way of vegetables. She was pretty good, but I was downright hopeless. I still remember my grandma trying to convince to "eat my greens," so I could be as strong as Popeye, but it would take a few more decades before I would eat my first leaf of spinach. One fateful evening when I was about 8 years old, my sister and I sat down to our favorite dinner of lamb chops only to find a small bowl of green beans in front of us. We asked where the lamb chops were and my mom pointed to the kitchen counter. She said, "Before you eat lamb chops, you must eat your green beans." I hated green beans even though I had never eaten them, but they now stood between me and my beloved lamb chops. I whined and begged, but nothing worked. My mom repeated, "Eat your green beans and you get your lamb chops." I had no choice, but I had a brilliant plan: If I put all the green beans in my mouth at once and washed them down with a big gulp of lemonade, then I would never taste them and it would be over in an instant. I was right. It was over in an instant, but not quite as planned. I knew I was in trouble when I saw my parents wiping string beans from their faces. To this day, I do not know exactly what happened, but somehow, my mouth full of green beans and pink lemonade ended up all over my parents. Like any resourceful child, I blamed my sister for making me laugh, but I was nonetheless banished to my bedroom without dinner – the worst punishment for an always-hungry child. My parents and sister love to tell this story, but it took me another 30 years before I ate another green bean and enjoyed it!

Given my education and career choice, I have seen decades of clear research on the health benefits of a diet rich in vegetables. It was impossible to ignore the proof that such a diet would reduce my lifelong risk of disease and provide benefits in terms of energy, longevity and quality of life. Under the weight of all the research, I gradually undid a lifetime of bad eating habits. Finally, I was eating healthy and felt great, but truth be told, I was not enjoying the food. Eating used to be fun. I had managed to change my old habits and I even became a vegan for a couple of years, but eating was no longer enjoyable. I was vibrantly healthy, but food was not fun. The turning point came when I was shown that healthy food was not just to be tolerated, but something you specifically created to be enjoyed. In other words, just because it's healthy does not mean it has to taste bad. In short, I was no longer a victim of a boring, healthy diet, but thriving on a rich, delicious diet comprised of healthy foods. Green beans, spinach, kale, Brussels sprouts, broccoli and cabbage were now things I looked forward to eating. Who knew? It was simply a matter of learning how to be responsible for making my healthy diet fun and enjoyable. Interestingly enough, my first step to eating much healthier were many of the vegetable-rich soups that were the subject of our first cookbook.

In this book our goal is to help you find healthy, nutritious, delicious dishes that you will enjoy preparing and eating. Just as eating badly always has its consequences; every time we eat well delivers long-term healthy dividends. This book is designed to abundantly deliver those dividends. Plus, it was not sufficient that a recipe be healthy to be included, it also had to taste so good that I loved eating it. There were dozens of healthy recipes I excluded, because they did not taste fantastic or were just too hard to prepare. I believe Muriel has succeeded brilliantly with all 45 recipes in this book. The pictures and instructions make them easy to follow and even if all you find are a few that you love, then the health benefits of those recipes will have been worth all our hard work.

Although I create vitamins, I have always said that even the best vitamins must take a back seat to a diet rich in vegetables and fruits. We all want to live as long as possible and we dream of preventing disease, and there is no better way to do so than by changing what we eat. There are no guarantees in life, but nothing is more certain to prevent disease and insure great health than a diet rich in nutritious vegetables. Personally, I am grateful I learned to prepare vegetables so that I can joyfully embrace all their enormous health benefits. Plus, it is never too late to do so. It took me almost 40 years to discover a healthier and more enjoyable way to eat, but now I get to reap the benefits over what will certainly be a longer, healthier and more active life.

You can do the same!

Best of health!

INTRODUCTION

As a result of a multitude of requests, and following the exceptionally positive response to our first cookbook (**Andrew's Favorite Soups for Wellness and Weight-loss**), Andrew and I have collaborated on a new cookbook designed to make it even easier for all of us to eat well. We answer the most common question we both receive: *How can eating healthy be more enjoyable?* This book responds by focusing on the foods that all of us know we *should* eat, but all of us consistently avoid eating because we never learned how to enjoy eating them.

Today, I eat a diet rich in vegetables, but it was not always that way. Being raised in Paris, France came with its own set of traditional dietary challenges. Every meal seemed to come with abundance of bread, butter, potatoes and cream-based sauces. Clearly, I would have been better served by being raised in the South of France where the healthy Mediterranean diet has its roots, but we all inherit the diet of our upbringing. And in order to achieve my best health, I would need to overcome the traditional eating habits of a typically Parisian family. Ironically, I have now adopted a more Mediterranean (and Asian) style of eating where vegetables are prepared with healthy spices and herbs to replace the non-nutritious calories of a more Parisian (and American) traditional diet. It was not easy to leave behind those old Parisian ways, but once I learned how to prepare things differently, I not only enjoyed, but preferred the flavor and textures of the healthier foods I prepared. Plus I always would feel better after having eaten them. And once you try just a few of the recipes in this book, I am confident that you will feel the same way.

Basically, my goal with this book is to help everyone discover what a pleasure it is both to prepare and eat extremely healthy vegetables like kale, collard greens, Swiss chard, Brussels sprouts, broccoli, cauliflower, cabbage, asparagus and more. These are by far the healthiest of foods, but for most Americans (and even Parisians) only rarely consumed. As Andrew always reminds me, it is impossible to overstate the impact of what we eat (both good and bad) on the current and future state of our health. This easy-to-follow cookbook is intended to provide an opportunity to transform our lives by making foods that protect our health a delicious and normal part of our daily routine.

Bon Appétit!

Muriel

CONTENTS

Cruciferous and Brassica Vegetables

KALE (Our Favorite)

Kale offers the most comprehensive nutrition of all the amazingly healthy cruciferous vegetables. Kale is low in calories and offers a uniquely rich combination of vitamins, minerals, fiber and phytonutrients, such as sulforaphane, indole-3-carbinol and other glucosinolates. It is also the most concentrated source of the eye-protective carotenoids lutein and zeaxanthin. Sadly, Kale is infrequently consumed in America, but these wonderful recipes should make it easy to enjoy the benefits of this astoundingly healthy food.

1
INCREDIBLE KALE, RED CABBAGE AND POMEGRANATE SALAD

4
MICHELLE'S KALE AND BRUSSELS SPROUTS CHOPPED SALAD

2
KALE WITH ROASTED BUTTERNUT SQUASH AND MARJORAM

5
KALE, RED CABBAGE AND ROASTED EGGPLANT

3
KALE TURKEY BURGERS

6
EGGPLANT PARMIGIANA WITH KALE

BRUSSELS SPROUTS

Brussels Sprouts are perhaps the least frequently consumed of the cruciferous vegetables, which is a pity given their rich content of protective nutrients. They look like "mini-Cabbage" and like other cruciferous vegetables, they are low in calories, while rich in vitamins, minerals, fiber and a wide array of beneficial and highly protective phytonutrients, including sulforaphane, indole-3-carbinol and other glucosinolates.

7
SAUTÉED BRUSSELS SPROUTS WITH ALMONDS

_____

9
BRUSSELS SPROUT *GRATIN*

_____

8
BRUSSELS SPROUTS SAUTÉED WITH SESAME SEEDS ASIAN STYLE

_____

CABBAGE

Cabbage is also a member of the cruciferous vegetable family and a wonderful substitute for less nutritious lettuce, such as iceberg. There are three main types of cabbage: green, red and Savoy. Like all of the cruciferous vegetables, cabbage is rich in vitamins, minerals, fiber and a wide array of beneficial and highly protective phytonutrients, including sulforaphane, indole-3-carbinol and other glucosinolates. Red cabbage also contains beneficial compounds called anthocyanins, which are also found in red grapes and red wine.

10
ANDREW'S FAVORITE CHOPPED CHICKEN AND CABBAGE SALAD

_____

12
VIETNAMESE CABBAGE SALAD

_____

11
SAVOY CABBAGE, WATERCRESS VEGGIE ROLLS

_____

13
SAVORY SALAD WITH RED CABBAGE AND PINEAPPLE

_____

BROCCOLI

Broccoli is perhaps the most well-known member of the cruciferous or brassica family of vegetables. Its name is Italian in origin and refers to the flowering top of a cabbage plant – a close relative of both broccoli and cauliflower. Broccoli is very low in calories while also rich in vitamins, minerals, fiber and a wide array of beneficial and highly protective phytonutrients, including sulforaphane, indole-3-carbinol and other glucosinolates.

14
BROCCOLI AND SHRIMP SAUTÉED WITH CHILI FLAKES & SHREDDED COCONUT

16
ANDREW'S FAVORITE GRILLED BROCCOLI

15
BROCCOLI "SOUFFLÉ"

17
BROCOLINI AND GREEN BEAN LETTUCE CUPS

CAULIFLOWER

Cauliflower is also a member of the cruciferous family with a shape and structure very similar to broccoli. Its name means cabbage flower and although typically white, cauliflower also comes in orange, green and purple varieties. Like broccoli, it is low in calories, while rich in vitamins, minerals, fiber and a wide array of protective phytonutrients, including sulforaphane, indole-3-carbinol and other glucosinolates. Like red cabbage, purple cauliflower contains protective anthocyanins like those found in red grapes and red wine.

18
ANDREW'S FAVORITE GRILLED CAULIFLOWER

20
ANDREW'S MASHED CAULIFLOWER

19
CAULIFLOWER CASSEROLE DE MA GRAND-MÈRE

21
CAULIFLOWER AND TOMATO CASSEROLE WITH ALMONDS AND PARMESAN

COLLARD GREENS

Collard greens are yet another member of the brassica and cruciferous family and are closely related to kale, cabbage and broccoli. They are dark green in color and rich in vitamins, minerals, fiber and protective phytonutrients, including sulforaphane and other glucosinolates. Also, like most green leafy vegetables, they are particularly rich in the protective carotenoids lutein and zeaxanthin.

22

EGG-WHITE FRITTATA WITH COLLARD GREENS, ZUCCHINI AND TURMERIC

23

COLLARD GREENS AND GREEN BEANS À L'ORANGE

WASABI

The healthy Asian diet offers numerous examples of how to eat better and wasabi is one of the most powerful – certainly in terms of flavor! It is referred to as Japanese Horseradish and is among the most popular Japanese spices. Like most pungent spices, wasabi is a rich source of protective compounds. It also happens to be a member of the Brassica family of vegetables being closely related to cabbage. Wasabi is prepared from the root of the plant and generally consumed in a dried powder or moist paste form. It's known for its potent, nasal-passage-permeating flavor and is most familiar to westerners when consumed with sushi. In the US you must be sure your wasabi is the real thing, since most US "wasabi" is a green-colored horseradish copy.

24

WASABI-WATERCRESS *"NUTTY HUMMUS"*

25

WASABI SMOKED SALMON GREEN BEAN ROLLS

Green Vegetables

ASPARAGUS

Asparagus resembles a greenish-purple (sometimes white) spear with a bud-like head. Each Asparagus spear is the non-woody, immature stem of the Asparagus plant and is closely related to the lily family. It is among the healthiest of vegetables containing a rich array of vitamins, minerals, phytonutrients, fiber and even protein – the latter accounts for the characteristic odor we might experience after eating Asparagus.

26
DICED ASPARAGUS, AVOCADO AND TOMATO TARTAR

27
ASPARAGUS BUNDLES IN PROSCIUTTO WITH PARMESAN

28
ASPARAGUS, SALMON AND BABY CORN ASIAN SAUTÉ

29
SAUTÉED ASPARAGUS TO "BRAGG" ABOUT

30
VERY GREEN ASPARAGUS RISOTTO

SWISS CHARD

Swiss Chard is a close relative of the beet, but as a green leafy vegetable, its exceptional nutrient content is concentrated in the leaf and not the root. Swiss Chard stalks come in a variety of colors and Rainbow Chard is the bundling together of these multicolored varieties. Swiss Chard is among the most nutritious of green leafy vegetables and offers a welcome change from less nutritious varieties of lettuce.

31
SWISS CHARD WITH SHIITAKE MUSHROOM

33
SWISS CHARD EGG-WHITE FRITTATA DE PROVENCE WITH FETA CHEESE

32
RAINBOW SWISS CHARD SAUTÉED WITH PINE NUTS AND DRIED APRICOTS

34
SWISS CHARD CASSEROLE WITH QUINOA AND TOMATOES

ZUCCHINI

Zucchini is perhaps the most frequently consumed and easily home-grown variety of squash. Like the Tomato, Zucchini is technically a fruit that is generally thought of as a vegetable. It looks quite similar to the cucumber and like the cucumber is edible in its entirety, including its skin, flesh and seeds. It possesses a remarkably low caloric content, along with high levels of key B-vitamins, minerals and carotenoids.

35
ZUCCHINI CASSEROLE WITH ALMONDS AND PARMESAN CHEESE

Colorful Vegetables (Fruits)

BELL PEPPERS

The Bell Pepper is a relative of the tomato and although both are considered vegetables from a culinary standpoint, technically and botanically, they are actually fruits. Bell Peppers may have been brought over and even named as peppers by Columbus, despite their lacking the hot, spicy taste of typical "peppers," since they do not contain capsaicin. They are rich in vitamins, such as vitamin C, and their remarkably bright colors are direct evidence of the rich complement of protective carotenoids they contain.

36
STUFFED BELL PEPPERS WITH MILLET, MUSHROOMS AND TURMERIC

39
BELL PEPPER AND SNOW PEAS SHRIMP PAD THAI

37
ROASTED BELL PEPPERS WITH OLIVES

40
LINDSEY'S STUFFED POBLANOS WITH QUINOA AND CHICKEN

38
BELL PEPPER TARTAR WITH POPPY SEEDS

41
RED BELL PEPPER "NUTTY HUMMUS"

TOMATOES

Tomatoes, like Bell Peppers, were brought to Europe in the 15th or 16th century by the earliest explorers of the New World – perhaps even Columbus. Tomatoes are now cultivated and consumed around the world. Like Bell Peppers, Tomatoes are technically fruits even though generally considered vegetables. Tomatoes are easily grown in home gardens and come in an infinite variety of shapes, sizes and colors. Nutritionally, they are most well-known for their high content of the exceptionally protective carotenoid – Lycopene.

42
TOMATO PROVENÇALE
À LA MURIEL

43
TOMATO MARINARA SAUCE

Healthy Spice

TURMERIC (Curry)

Turmeric has been cultivated throughout Asia for over 5,000 years. It has been viewed by both traditional Chinese and Indian medicine as possessing a long list of health benefits. Modern science has now validated many of these benefits and as a result, Andrew has used it in his products for more than 20 years. Turmeric is a close relative of ginger and both are derived from a rhizome-like root structure. Turmeric's rich flavor and deep yellow color make it the most characteristic ingredient in curry.

44
TURMERIC CURRY OF
PINEAPPLE WITH CARROTS,
COCONUT AND CINNAMON

45
TURMERIC COCONUT CURRY
OF SWEET POTATO WITH
ENGLISH PEAS AND TOFU

INCREDIBLE KALE, RED CABBAGE AND POMEGRANATE SALAD

8 – 10 CUPS • PREPARATION: 10 MINUTES • COOKING: 0 MINUTES • MEDIUM

Andrew long ago fell in love with kale's incredibly rich nutrient content, but he struggled to enjoy eating it. Not anymore. This is one incredibly delicious and good-for-you salad. Andrew can't get enough of it. You can also replace the pomegranate with dried cranberries and the lemon juice with pomegranate juice. Kale is amazingly nutritious. We eat kale virtually every day. It is low in calories and delivers an unparalleled array of protective phytonutrients. Red cabbage is a healthy cruciferous vegetable that is uniquely rich in the anthocyanins found in red wine or red grapes. Best of all, this salad tastes just as good as it is rich in nutrition.

4 packed cups curly kale, minced

¼ head red cabbage (2 cups), finely shredded

Sea Salt to taste

¾ cup roasted pine nuts

½ cup Parmesan cheese, shredded

½ cup pomegranate seeds

Juice of 1 large lemon

3 tbsp. olive oil

Pepper to taste

1 In a large bowl, add the kale, cabbage and sea salt and let it rest for 5 minutes, allowing it to "sweat."

2 Meanwhile, in a small bowl, whisk the lemon juice with pepper and olive oil.

3 In the bowl with the kale/cabbage mix, add the pine nuts, Parmesan cheese, pomegranate seeds and dressing. Salt and pepper to taste. Mix all ingredients together.

Nutrition Information

Serving Size **1 Cup**   Servings **10**

Calories	**131**	Potassium	**192 mg**
Calories from fat	**102**	Total Carbohydrates	**6 g**
Total Fat	**11 g**	Dietary Fiber	**1 g**
Cholesterol	**3 mg**	Sugars	**3 g**
Sodium	**77 mg**	Protein	**4 g**

Vitamin A	**25 %**	Folic Acid	**4 %**
Vitamin C	**42 %**	Vitamin B12	**1 %**
Calcium	**8 %**	Pantothenic Acid	**1 %**
Iron	**5 %**	Phosphorus	**11 %**
Vitamin E	**7 %**	Magnesium	**9 %**
Vitamin K	**108 %**	Zinc	**6 %**
Vitamin B1	**5 %**	Selenium	**2 %**
Vitamin B2	**4 %**	Copper	**15 %**
Niacin	**3 %**	Manganese	**51 %**
Vitamin B6	**5 %**		

OTHER BENEFICIAL NUTRIENTS (PER SERVING)

Choline	**11 mg**
Beta-Carotene	**717 mcg**
Alpha-Carotene	**5 mcg**
Lutein & Zeaxanthin	**880 mcg**
Lycopene	**4 mcg**

KALE WITH ROASTED BUTTERNUT SQUASH AND MARJORAM

8 CUPS • PREPARATION: 20 MINUTES • COOKING: 20 MINUTES • MEDIUM

Another delicious way to enjoy the health benefits of kale. Oddly enough, the most difficult part of this recipe is cutting the squash, but many supermarkets offer pre-cut squash, which will make this recipe a breeze. If you cannot find fresh marjoram, you can replace it with fresh thyme. I really love the way marjoram works here, so if you can't find it locally, you can always order it online.

4 cups kale packed (6 oz. bunch),
   finely chopped

3 cups butternut squash, cubed

1 medium red onion, chopped

2 cloves garlic, minced

1 oz. fresh marjoram (or thyme)

½ cup pumpkin seeds

Salt and pepper to taste

1 tbsp. olive oil
   (or olive oil spray)

1 Preheat the oven to 375°. Spread a sheet of parchment paper or tin foil on a cookie sheet. Add the butternut squash and spray with a little olive oil, add a pinch of salt and pepper. Roast for 20 minutes.

2 During this time, in a large pan over medium heat, add remaining olive oil and the chopped kale, onion and garlic. Sauté for 5 minutes. Add the pumpkin seeds and marjoram without the stem, and a pinch of salt and pepper. Add the cooked butternut squash and mix everything together.

3   Serve warm as an appetizer or side dish.

Nutrition Information

Serving Size **1 Cup**		Servings **8**

Calories **106**	Potassium . . . . . . **388 mg**	
Calories from fat **27**	Total Carbohydrates . . . **12 g**	
Total Fat . . . . **3 g**	Dietary Fiber . . . . **3 g**	
Cholesterol . . . . **0 mg**	Sugars . . . . **2 g**	
Sodium . . . . **11 mg**	Protein . . . . **4 g**	

Vitamin A . . . . . . **142 %**	Vitamin B6 . . . . **10 %**		
Vitamin C . . . . **49 %**	Folic Acid . . . . **9 %**		
Calcium . . . . **10 %**	Pantothenic Acid . . . . **3 %**		
Iron . . . . **23 %**	Phosphorus . . . . **14 %**		
Vitamin E . . . . **6 %**	Magnesium . . . . **21 %**		
Vitamin K . . . . . **139 %**	Zinc . . . . **6 %**		
Vitamin B1 . . . . **7 %**	Selenium . . . . **2 %**		
Vitamin B2 . . . . **3 %**	Copper . . . . **19 %**		
Niacin . . . . **7 %**	Manganese . . . . **39 %**		

OTHER BENEFICIAL NUTRIENTS (PER SERVING)

Choline . . . . **8 mg**
Beta-Carotene . . . . **3,129 mcg**
Alpha-Carotene . . . . **445 mcg**
Lutein & Zeaxanthin . . . . **1,098 mcg**

KALE TURKEY BURGERS

12 - 15 MINI-BURGERS • PREPARATION: 15 MINUTES • COOKING: 15 MINUTES • MEDIUM

Andrew loves these and, since I make them as mini-burgers, he eats them as finger food with our Tomato Marinara Sauce (Recipe #43). Andrew loves the fact that he is eating kale while enjoying the healthy lean protein from the turkey. I usually serve these mini-burgers on a bed of watercress. We used to make them with mushrooms, but I added kale to make them even healthier and I will still sometimes add back the mushrooms as well. As with all my recipes, feel free to make them your own by adding and subtracting ingredients as you see fit.

1 lb. ground turkey	1 egg	2 tbsp. canola oil
1 large shallot or small red onion	1 tsp. paprika	2 cups watercress to serve
2 cloves garlic	1 tsp. cumin	Marinara Sauce (optional)
3 large kale leaves (1½ cups), deveined	1 tsp. crushed chili pepper	(Recipe #43)
	Salt and pepper to taste	

1 In a large bowl, mix all the ingredients (except for the canola oil): ground turkey, chopped shallots, minced garlic, finely chopped kale, egg, paprika, cumin, chili pepper, salt and pepper. I mix everything by hand.

2 Form the mini–burgers (approximately 12 to 15).

3 In a warm pan, add canola oil and cook the burgers for approximately 7 minutes on each side over medium heat.

4 Serve on a bed of watercress with Marinara Sauce (Recipe #43) on the side.

Nutrition Information

Serving Size **2 Mini Burgers**   Servings **6**

Calories **177**	Potassium . . . . . . **342 mg**
Calories from fat **96**	Total Carbohydrates . . . . **5 g**
Total Fat . . . . **11 g**	Dietary Fiber . . . . **1 g**
Cholesterol . . . . . **83 mg**	Sugars . . . . **1 g**
Sodium . . . . **74 mg**	Protein . . . . **16 g**

Vitamin A . . . . **49 %**	Vitamin B6 . . . . . . **20 %**
Vitamin C . . . . **42 %**	Folic Acid . . . . **5 %**
Calcium . . . . **6 %**	Vitamin B12 . . . . . . **16 %**
Iron . . . . **10 %**	Pantothenic Acid . . . . **9 %**
Vitamin D3 . . . . **4 %**	Phosphorus . . . . **19 %**
Vitamin E . . . . **6 %**	Magnesium . . . . **8 %**
Vitamin K . . . . . . **151 %**	Zinc . . . . **15 %**
Vitamin B1 . . . . **6 %**	Selenium . . . . **25 %**
Vitamin B2 . . . . **13 %**	Copper . . . . **18 %**
Niacin . . . . **22 %**	Manganese . . . . **11 %**

OTHER BENEFICIAL NUTRIENTS (PER SERVING)

Choline	**65 mg**
Beta-Carotene	**1,363 mcg**
Alpha-Carotene	**11 mcg**
Lutein & Zeaxanthin	**1,904 mcg**

MICHELLE'S KALE AND BRUSSELS SPROUTS CHOPPED SALAD

10 CUPS • PREPARATION: 15 MINUTES • COOKING: 0 MINUTES • MEDIUM

Our friend, Michelle, is a wonderful chef who makes a delicious raw kale and Brussels sprouts salad. I was so impressed and inspired with this healthy salad that I had to make it part of our Healthy Veggies cookbook. Kale, Brussels sprouts and almonds are three of Andrew's and my favorite, healthy super-foods. This salad has them all, which makes it so nutritionally rich and ideally balanced. Best of all, is how amazingly delicious you will find this salad to be.

4 cups kale, packed (6 oz. bunch)

3 cups Brussels sprouts, chopped

Pinch of sea salt

1½ cups sliced almonds

1 cup Parmesan cheese, shaved

1 oz. fresh cilantro

For the dressing:

3 tbsp. olive oil

1 tbsp. Dijon mustard

3 tbsp. lemon juice

Salt and pepper to taste

1 Wash the kale and finely chop in a food processor. Reserve in a bowl. Wash the Brussels sprouts, remove the ends and finely chop in the food processor. Place in the bowl with the kale and sea salt to make it sweat.

2 Make the dressing by whisking together the olive oil, mustard, lemon juice, salt and pepper.

3 Dry roast the almonds in a pan for approximately 5 minutes over medium-low heat until they are a golden color. Chop the cilantro finely.

4 In the bowl with the kale and Brussels sprouts, add the cheese, almonds, dressing and cilantro.

5 Mix well and serve in small salad bowls of your choosing.

Nutrition Information

Serving Size **1 Cup**   Servings **10**

Calories	**172**	Potassium	**341 mg**
Calories from fat	**116**	Total Carbohydrates	**9 g**
Total Fat	**13 g**	Dietary Fiber	**3 g**
Cholesterol	**7 mg**	Sugars	**2 g**
Sodium	**203 mg**	Protein	**9 g**

Vitamin A	**29 %**	Folic Acid	**10 %**
Vitamin C	**87 %**	Vitamin B12	**2 %**
Calcium	**20 %**	Pantothenic Acid	**3 %**
Iron	**8 %**	Phosphorus	**18 %**
Vitamin E	**22 %**	Magnesium	**15 %**
Vitamin K	**191 %**	Zinc	**7 %**
Vitamin B1	**8 %**	Selenium	**6 %**
Vitamin B2	**14 %**	Copper	**16 %**
Niacin	**5 %**	Manganese	**27 %**
Vitamin B6	**8 %**		

OTHER BENEFICIAL NUTRIENTS (PER SERVING)

Choline	**18 mg**
Beta-Carotene	**805 mcg**
Alpha-Carotene	**8 mcg**
Lutein & Zeaxanthin	**1,534 mcg**

KALE, RED CABBAGE AND ROASTED EGGPLANT

10 CUPS • PREPARATION: 15 MINUTES • COOKING: 17 MINUTES • MEDIUM

It is hard to imagine anything healthier than a recipe that combines kale and red cabbage. Plus, it only gets better when you add the wonderfully filling texture and low calorie goodness of eggplant. Andrew really enjoys this when I combine it with a little bit of diced chicken or tofu. Some folks might enjoy this over brown rice, but we prefer it over a "non-grain" such as quinoa or with a legume, such as barley or lentils.

1 tbsp. olive oil	¼ head red cabbage (2 cups chopped)	1 tsp. Sriracha (or red chili flakes)
2 cloves garlic, minced	½ bunch kale (3 cups chopped)	1 tbsp. sesame seeds
4 cups eggplant (3 Japanese or 1 regular), sliced	½ cup raisins	½ cup green onions
Salt to taste	Juice of 1 lime	

1 In a large skillet over medium heat, add the olive oil, garlic and sliced eggplant with a little salt. Cook for 5 minutes. Remove from pan and reserve.

2 In the same skillet, add the chopped red cabbage and cook for 5 minutes over medium heat.

3 On top of the cooked cabbage, add the kale and raisins, and cook for an additional 3 to 5 minutes.

4 Combine lime juice, Sriracha, salt and sesame seeds. Mix with the eggplant and cook everything together for 2 more minutes, so the flavors mix. Serve garnished with green onions.

Nutrition Information

Serving Size **1 Cup** Servings **10**

Calories	**68**	Potassium	**261 mg**
Calories from fat	**23**	Total Carbohydrates	**14 g**
Total Fat	**3 g**	Dietary Fiber	**2 g**
Cholesterol	**0 mg**	Sugars	**7 g**
Sodium	**11 mg**	Protein	**2 g**

Vitamin A	**28 %**	Vitamin B6	**7 %**
Vitamin C	**40 %**	Folic Acid	**4 %**
Calcium	**4 %**	Pantothenic Acid	**2 %**
Iron	**5 %**	Phosphorus	**4 %**
Vitamin E	**3 %**	Magnesium	**4 %**
Vitamin K	**100 %**	Zinc	**2 %**
Vitamin B1	**4 %**	Selenium	**2 %**
Vitamin B2	**3 %**	Copper	**13 %**
Niacin	**3 %**	Manganese	**16 %**

OTHER BENEFICIAL NUTRIENTS (PER SERVING)

Choline	**7 mg**
Beta-Carotene	**816 mcg**
Alpha-Carotene	**5 mcg**
Lutein & Zeaxanthin	**938 mcg**
Lycopene	**4 mcg**

EGGPLANT PARMIGIANA WITH KALE

12 CUPS • PREPARATION: 40 MINUTES • COOKING: 20 MINUTES • DIFFICULT & LONG

I had to convince Andrew to include this recipe, since it is a bit higher in calories than the others, but he loves the use of kale and its abundance of key nutrients. Plus, Andrew is the first to admit that this dish is absolutely delicious. We usually only make it for special occasions and serve it in small portions as a yummy side dish. We did just that when we recently celebrated my American citizenship. I do not add any salt, since we salt the eggplant at the start to make it "sweat." Surprisingly, eggplant is technically a fruit that is closely related to another nutritious fruit in this recipe - the tomato.

1 large (approx. 1 lb.) eggplant

1 pinch salt

1½ cups (3 leaves) kale

⅓ cup garbanzo flour

1 cup egg whites

½ cup olive oil

2 cups Marinara Sauce
(Recipe #43) or your
favorite store-bought brand

1 garlic clove

16 oz. fresh mozzarella cheese

1 cup Parmesan cheese, shredded

Salt and pepper to taste

1 oz. fresh basil

1 Preheat the oven to 375°. Slice the eggplant and add a pinch of salt on the top. Let it rest on a paper towel, allowing it to "sweat."

2 Mince the kale very finely. Reserve.

3 With the garbanzo flour on a plate and the egg whites in a bowl, coat the eggplant slices LIGHTLY with flour and then dip in the egg whites.

4 Place a large skillet on high heat and add half the olive oil. Reduce the heat to medium and sauté the eggplant for about 5 minutes on each side.

5 Remove and let rest on a paper towel. Repeat the operation until all the eggplant is done. This takes a little while (approximately 25 minutes).

6 Rub garlic clove over a 9" x 9" baking dish and leave in dish. Spread ¼ cup of Marinara Sauce (Recipe #43) on the bottom of the dish, followed by grilled eggplant, minced kale, sliced mozzarella and half of the Parmesan. Pepper to taste.

7 Repeat the layers and cover top layer completely with the remaining Marinara Sauce (approx. 1 cup), mozzarella and Parmesan cheese. Bake for 20 minutes.

8 Finely chop the basil and sprinkle it over the casserole before serving.

Nutrition Information

Serving Size **1 Cup**   Servings **12**

Calories **248**	Potassium . . . . . . **411 mg**
Calories from fat . . . **157**	Total Carbohydrates . . . **11 g**
Total Fat . . . . **17 g**	Dietary Fiber . . . . **3 g**
Cholesterol . . . . . **36 mg**	Sugars . . . . **5 g**
Sodium . . . . **619 mg**	Protein . . . . **15 g**

Vitamin A . . . . **33 %**	Vitamin B6. . . . . . . **10 %**
Vitamin C . . . . **21 %**	Folic Acid. . . . . **7 %**
Calcium . . . . **31 %**	Vitamin B12 . . . . . . **16 %**
Iron . . . . **6 %**	Pantothenic Acid . . . . **3 %**
Vitamin D3. . . . . **2 %**	Phosphorus. . . . . . . **24 %**
Vitamin E. . . . . **12 %**	Magnesium. . . . . . . **10 %**
Vitamin K . . . . . . **104 %**	Zinc . . . . **11 %**
Vitamin B1. . . . . **5 %**	Selenium . . . . **22 %**
Vitamin B2. . . . . . . **17 %**	Copper . . . . **12 %**
Niacin . . . . **14 %**	Manganese . . . . **21 %**

OTHER BENEFICIAL NUTRIENTS (PER SERVING)

Choline. . . . . **19 mg**
Beta-Carotene. . . . . **821 mcg**
Alpha-Carotene . . . . **5 mcg**
Lutein & Zeaxanthin. . . . . **936 mcg**
Lycopene. . . . . **6,966 mcg**

SAUTÉED BRUSSELS SPROUTS WITH ALMONDS

7 - 8 CUPS • PREPARATION: 10 MINUTES • COOKING: 12 MINUTES • EASY

Andrew can't believe how much he enjoys Brussels sprouts after spending almost his entire life avoiding them. They are without question among the healthiest and most protective foods you can consume. The addition of almonds provides a wonderful crunchy texture that Andrew loves and is a great source of protein, healthy fats and fiber.

½ cup almonds, sliced

2 tbsp. olive oil

2 lbs. Brussels sprouts, quartered

2 garlic cloves, minced

1 shallot, chopped

Salt and pepper to taste

Fresh thyme, a few sprigs

1 In a small pan over medium heat, sauté the almonds for 2 to 3 minutes until golden. Reserve.

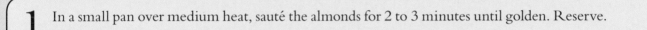

2 In a large pan over medium to high heat, add the olive oil, Brussels sprouts, garlic, shallots, salt and pepper. Cook for about 4 to 5 minutes until golden. Reduce heat, cover and finish cooking for another 4 to 5 minutes. The Brussels sprouts should be a bright green color.

3 Add the thyme. Sprinkle the almonds on top and serve immediately.

Nutrition Information

Serving Size **1 Cup**   Servings **8**

Calories **104**		Potassium . . . . . . **489 mg**
Calories from fat **49**		Total Carbohydrates . . . **12 g**
Total Fat . . . . **5 g**		Dietary Fiber . . . . **5 g**
Cholesterol . . . . **0 mg**		Sugars . . . . **3 g**
Sodium . . . . **29 mg**		Protein . . . . **5 g**

Vitamin A . . . . **17 %**		Folic Acid . . . . **18 %**
Vitamin C . . . . . . **161 %**		Pantothenic Acid . . . . **4 %**
Calcium . . . . **6 %**		Phosphorus . . . . **11 %**
Iron . . . . **10 %**		Magnesium . . . . **10 %**
Vitamin E . . . . **14 %**		Zinc . . . . **4 %**
Vitamin K . . . . . . **253 %**		Selenium . . . . **3 %**
Vitamin B1 . . . . **11 %**		Copper . . . . **7 %**
Vitamin B2 . . . . **9 %**		Manganese . . . . **26 %**
Niacin . . . . **5 %**		
Vitamin B6 . . . . **14 %**		

OTHER BENEFICIAL NUTRIENTS (PER SERVING)

Choline	**25 mg**
Beta-Carotene	**510 mcg**
Alpha-Carotene	**7 mcg**
Lutein & Zeaxanthin	**1,803 mcg**

BRUSSELS SPROUTS SAUTÉED WITH SESAME SEEDS ASIAN STYLE

7 CUPS • PREPARATION: 10 MINUTES • COOKING: 10 MINUTES • EASY

This Asian-inspired recipe is slightly spicy from the ginger and red chili flakes, but you can always make changes to keep your taste buds happy. Andrew is still surprised that another Brussels sprouts recipe is among his favorites. The warm flavors from the Asian spices and the crunchy addition of sesame seeds make this not only a delicious treat, but an exceptionally rich source of protective phytonutrients.

2 lbs. Brussels sprouts	2 cloves of garlic, minced	1 tbsp. low-sodium soy sauce
1 tbsp. dark sesame oil	1 tbsp. ginger, grated	1 tsp. red chili pepper flakes
1 tbsp. agave or honey	½ cup raisins	1 tbsp. dark or white sesame seeds

1 Wash the Brussels sprouts and cut them in half. If some are too big, cut them in quarters. Steam for 3 minutes.

2 In a large pan over medium to high heat, add the sesame oil, agave, garlic, ginger, raisins and Brussels sprouts. Sauté for approximately 5 minutes until crisp, golden and tender. (Start with a high heat and then decrease to medium).

3 Add the soy sauce, red chili flakes and sesame seeds. Serve immediately as a side dish.

Nutrition Information

Serving Size **1 Cup**   Servings **7**

Calories	**118**	Potassium	**622 mg**
Calories from fat	**17**	Total Carbohydrates	**25 g**
Total Fat	**2 g**	Dietary Fiber	**6 g**
Cholesterol	**0 mg**	Sugars	**12 g**
Sodium	**111 mg**	Protein	**5 g**

Vitamin A	**25 %**	Folic Acid	**20 %**
Vitamin C	**185 %**	Pantothenic Acid	**4 %**
Calcium	**8 %**	Phosphorus	**12 %**
Iron	**13 %**	Magnesium	**10 %**
Vitamin E	**7 %**	Zinc	**5 %**
Vitamin K	**288 %**	Selenium	**4 %**
Vitamin B1	**14 %**	Copper	**9 %**
Vitamin B2	**9 %**	Manganese	**27 %**
Niacin	**6 %**		
Vitamin B6	**17 %**		

OTHER BENEFICIAL NUTRIENTS (PER SERVING)

Choline	**28 mg**
Beta-Carotene	**724 mcg**
Alpha-Carotene	**8 mcg**
Lutein & Zeaxanthin	**2,145 mcg**

Brussels Sprout Gratin

4 CUPS • PREPARATION: 20 MINUTES • COOKING: 20 MINUTES • DIFFICULT

Even if you don't normally like Brussels sprouts (like Andrew), you will fall in love with this dish. It is also a great opportunity to use small, oven-safe serving dishes (ramekins) or storage bowls (we do so with all our recipes), since that is the most reliable way to control portions. Even healthy foods can be abused and we have found that pre-measured portions are a foolproof means of avoiding overeating.

12 oz. Brussels sprouts

1 small red onion or shallot,
   finely chopped

¾ cup ricotta

2 large eggs, beaten

½ lemon

¾ cup shredded
   Parmesan cheese

Pinch each salt and
   cayenne pepper

4 sprigs thyme

1 tbsp. butter

1 Preheat oven to 375°. Wash the Brussels sprouts, cut them in halves, remove the ugly leaves. Steam for 3 minutes and strain.

2 During this time, start sautéing the chopped onion with butter in a pan over medium heat for 5 minutes.

3 Prepare the lemon zest and set aside. In a bowl mix together the sautéed onion, Ricotta, eggs, lemon, Parmesan cheese, salt, cayenne pepper and thyme. Mix in the Brussels sprouts and add the lemon zest.

4 Pour the mixture into a buttered baking dish or ramekins - not too full, as it will rise during baking. Bake for 20 minutes. Serve warm.

Nutrition Information

Serving Size **1 Cup**		Servings **4**
Calories **247**	Potassium . . . . . . **487 mg**	
Calories from fat . . . **137**	Total Carbohydrates . . . **13 g**	
Total Fat . . . . **15 g**	Dietary Fiber . . . . **4 g**	
Cholesterol . . . **133 mg**	Sugars . . . . **3 g**	
Sodium . . . . . . **371 mg**	Protein . . . . **17 g**	

Vitamin A . . . . **33 %**	Vitamin B6 . . . . **16 %**	
Vitamin C . . . . . . **130 %**	Folic Acid . . . . **19 %**	
Calcium . . . . **34 %**	Vitamin B12 . . . . . . **10 %**	
Iron . . . . **12 %**	Pantothenic Acid . . . . **9 %**	
Vitamin D3 . . . . **7 %**	Phosphorus . . . . **30 %**	
Vitamin E . . . . **8 %**	Magnesium . . . . **10 %**	
Vitamin K . . . . . **191 %**	Zinc . . . . **12 %**	
Vitamin B1 . . . . . . **10 %**	Selenium . . . . **28 %**	
Vitamin B2 . . . . . . **21 %**	Copper . . . . **5 %**	
Niacin . . . . **4 %**	Manganese . . . . . . **17 %**	

OTHER BENEFICIAL NUTRIENTS (PER SERVING)

Choline	**103 mg**
Beta-Carotene	**659 mcg**
Alpha-Carotene	**5 mcg**
Lutein & Zeaxanthin	**1,627 mcg**

ANDREW'S FAVORITE CHOPPED CHICKEN AND CABBAGE SALAD

10 CUPS • PREPARATION: 20 MINUTES • COOKING: 15 – 20 MINUTES • MEDIUM

Andrew adores this salad. We were trying to reinvent a healthier version of a salad from a local restaurant and we came up with something even tastier. The most important changes were to replace all the lettuce with raw, healthy cabbage and also replace the cream-based dressing with a delicious and healthy avocado dressing. The result is a true taste treat for Andrew.

2 chicken breasts (8 oz. ea.)

2½ cups cabbage, finely chopped

1 can (15 oz.) corn

2 cups cherry tomatoes, halved

½ cup scallions or green onions

1 can (15 oz.) low-sodium black beans, drained and rinsed

For the dressing:

1 large, ripe avocado (or 2 small)

¼ to ½ cup water

1 lime or 2 tbsp. lime juice

½ tsp. chipotle seasoning

1 tsp. agave

¼ cup cilantro

Salt and pepper to taste

1 In a pan on medium heat, sauté the chicken breasts until cooked through, approximately 7 minutes on each side depending on the thickness of the breast.

2 Chop the cooked chicken into bit-size squares. Reserve.

3 In a blender, combine the avocado, water, lime juice, chipotle seasoning, agave and cilantro. Mix well until smooth. Salt and pepper to taste.

4 In a salad bowl, combine the cabbage, corn, tomatoes, green onions, beans and chicken.

5 Mix well with the dressing and serve immediately. Decorate individual servings with a cilantro leaf.

Nutrition Information

Serving Size **1 Cup**   Servings **10**

Calories **258**	Potassium . . . . . . **717 mg**
Calories from fat **96**	Total Carbohydrates . . . **33 g**
Total Fat . . . . **11 g**	Dietary Fiber . . . . **7 g**
Cholesterol . . . . . . **19 mg**	Sugars . . . . **4 g**
Sodium . . . . **234 mg**	Protein . . . . **13 g**

Vitamin A . . . . **8 %**	Folic Acid. . . . . **37 %**
Vitamin C . . . . **26 %**	Vitamin B12 . . . . **2 %**
Calcium . . . . **6 %**	Pantothenic Acid . . . **10 %**
Iron . . . . **13 %**	Phosphorus. . . . . . . **22 %**
Vitamin E. . . . . **4 %**	Magnesium. . . . . . . **17 %**
Vitamin K . . . . **54 %**	Zinc . . . . **11 %**
Vitamin B1. . . . . . . **24 %**	Selenium . . . . **18 %**
Vitamin B2. . . . . . . **8 %**	Copper . . . . **20 %**
Niacin . . . . **19 %**	Manganese . . . . **29 %**
Vitamin B6. . . . . . . **10 %**	

OTHER BENEFICIAL NUTRIENTS (PER SERVING)

Choline.	**70 mg**
Beta-Carotene.	**203 mcg**
Alpha-Carotene	**42 mcg**
Lutein & Zeaxanthin.	**158 mcg**
Lycopene.	**767 mcg**

SAVOY CABBAGE, WATERCRESS VEGGIE ROLLS

10 - 12 ROLLS • PREPARATION: 20 MINUTES • COOKING: 0 MINUTES • MEDIUM

These are quick and easy and require no cooking at all. They are deliciously healthy and make the perfect light snack or appetizer. Cabbage contains remarkable levels of protective phytonutrients and is also incredibly low in calories at less than 20 calories per quarter pound. Watercress is the perfect addition to this ultra-low calorie, nutrient-packed appetizer, snack or side dish. You will find a million uses for the Red Bell Pepper "Nutty Hummus" (Recipe #41), which we use as the perfect sauce for these delicious veggie rolls.

5 or 6 Savoy cabbage leaves	1 large, ripe avocado	Red Bell Pepper "*Nutty Hummus*" (Recipe #41)
1 bell pepper (any color)	1 cup watercress, leave some of the stem	
½ cucumber		Toothpicks
	1 pack (1 oz.) fresh mint leaves	

1 Wash the Savoy cabbage, Julienne (thinly slice) the pepper and cucumber; remove the skin from the avocado and cut up; wash the watercress and prepare the mint leaves by removing the stems.

2 In a cabbage leaf, first spread a tbsp. of Red Bell Pepper "*Nutty Hummus*," then place a few strips of pepper, a piece of avocado, a few strips of cucumber, a few mint leaves and a little watercress. Roll the leaf a little tight being careful to not overstuff. Hold closed with a couple of toothpicks.

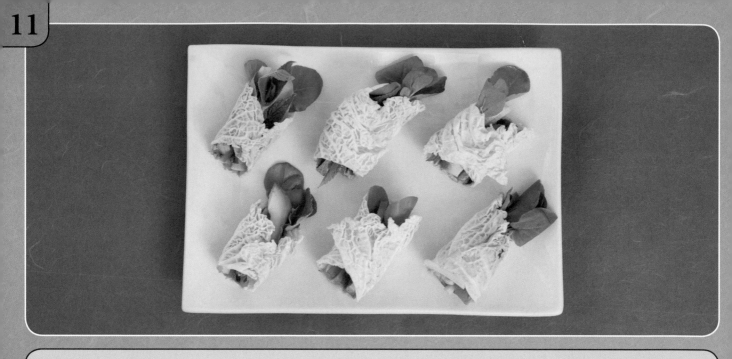

3 Cut the rolls in half and place on a serving plate. You may serve it with additional Red Bell Pepper "*Nutty Hummus*" on the side, as well.

Nutrition Information

Serving Size **1 Roll**   Servings **12**

Calories	**36**	Potassium	**194 mg**
Calories from fat	**23**	Total Carbohydrates	**3 g**
Total Fat	**3 g**	Dietary Fiber	**2 g**
Cholesterol	**0 mg**	Sugars	**1 g**
Sodium	**13 mg**	Protein	**1 g**

Vitamin A	**24 %**	Vitamin B6	**6 %**
Vitamin C	**46 %**	Folic Acid	**6 %**
Calcium	**3 %**	Pantothenic Acid	**4 %**
Iron	**2 %**	Phosphorus	**2 %**
Vitamin E	**4 %**	Magnesium	**3 %**
Vitamin K	**68 %**	Zinc	**1 %**
Vitamin B1	**3 %**	Copper	**3 %**
Vitamin B2	**4 %**	Manganese	**5 %**
Niacin	**2 %**		

OTHER BENEFICIAL NUTRIENTS (PER SERVING)

Choline	**6 mg**
Beta-Carotene	**693 mcg**
Alpha-Carotene	**6 mcg**
Lutein & Zeaxanthin	**1,140 mcg**

VIETNAMESE CABBAGE SALAD

8 – 10 CUPS • PREPARATION: 15 MINUTES • COOKING: 0 MINUTES • MEDIUM

This nutritious lovely salad is wonderfully light, fresh and extremely low in calories. It is one of my favorites to snack on throughout the day and Andrew likes it even more when I replace the tofu with a little bit of shrimp or chicken. The Vietnamese-inspired flavors make this low-calorie salad a treat for the taste buds and a protective gift for our bodies.

3 cups Chinese cabbage, minced

1 cup cucumber, peeled and
    cubed

1 cup mini carrots, thinly sliced

1 cup radish, thinly sliced

1 cup smoked tofu, cubed

½ cup cashews,
    lightly browned

1 oz. mint, minced

For the dressing

Juice of 3 limes

2 tbsp. fish sauce

1 tbsp. agave or honey

1 tbsp. ginger, minced

1 small red chili, minced

1   In a large bowl, add the cabbage, cucumber, carrots, radishes and tofu.

2   In a small bowl, mix the lime juice, fish sauce, agave, ginger and red chili.

3 Pour the dressing on top of the ingredients in the large bowl and add the nuts and minced mint. Toss well.

4 Serve in individual bowls decorated with a mint leaf.

Nutrition Information

Serving Size **1 Cup**   Servings **10**

Calories	85	Potassium	248 mg
Calories from fat	40	Total Carbohydrates	9 g
Total Fat	4 g	Dietary Fiber	1 g
Cholesterol	0 mg	Sugars	4 g
Sodium	882 mg	Protein	4 g

Vitamin A	60 %	Vitamin B6	7 %
Vitamin C	27 %	Folic Acid	8 %
Calcium	12 %	Pantothenic Acid	2 %
Iron	12 %	Phosphorus	9 %
Vitamin E	1 %	Magnesium	10 %
Vitamin K	19 %	Zinc	5 %
Vitamin B1	4 %	Selenium	5 %
Vitamin B2	4 %	Copper	12 %
Niacin	4 %	Manganese	16 %

OTHER BENEFICIAL NUTRIENTS (PER SERVING)

Choline	13 mg
Beta-Carotene	1,583 mcg
Alpha-Carotene	425 mcg
Lutein & Zeaxanthin	45 mcg

SAVORY SALAD WITH
RED CABBAGE AND PINEAPPLE

6 CUPS • PREPARATION: 20 MINUTES • COOKING: 0 MINUTES • EASY

For years, I played with the idea of mixing red cabbage with fruits such as pineapple or papaya and this wonderful salad is the happy (and healthy) result. Andrew has always reminded me that red cabbage is a cruciferous packed with special benefits, since it also contains the anthocyanins that make red wine and red grapes so healthy. Unfortunately, the taste of red cabbage does not appeal to everyone, particularly Andrew; but, now with the sweet addition of the bromelain-rich pineapple, even Andrew loves this salad.

½ head red cabbage
    (4 cups, max.)

Pinch of sea salt (optional)

2 cups pineapple, cubed

1 tbsp. olive oil

2 tbsp. apple juice

1 tbsp. apple cider vinegar

1 oz. chives, chopped

Pepper to taste

½ tsp. cumin

1 Remove any ugly leaves from the cabbage and chop into small pieces. Place in a bowl and add the sea salt, mixing well. Let it rest for a few minutes, allowing it to "sweat."

2 During this time, cut the pineapple into small squares. Add to the bowl with the red cabbage.

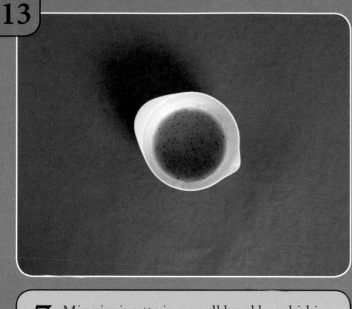

3 Mix vinaigrette in a small bowl by whisking the olive oil, juice, vinegar, chives, pepper and cumin.

4 Pour on top of the cabbage and pineapple, and mix well.

Nutrition Information

Serving Size **1 Cup**   Servings **6**

Calories	68	Potassium	223 mg
Calories from fat	22	Total Carbohydrates	11 g
Total Fat	2 g	Dietary Fiber	2 g
Cholesterol	0 mg	Sugars	8 g
Sodium	17 mg	Protein	1 g
Vitamin A	18 %	Vitamin B6	10 %
Vitamin C	105 %	Folic Acid	6 %
Calcium	4 %	Pantothenic Acid	2 %
Iron	5 %	Phosphorus	3 %
Vitamin E	2 %	Magnesium	4 %
Vitamin K	43 %	Zinc	2 %
Vitamin B1	6 %	Selenium	1 %
Vitamin B2	4 %	Copper	4 %
Niacin	3 %	Manganese	34 %

OTHER BENEFICIAL NUTRIENTS (PER SERVING)

Choline . . . . **13 mg**
Beta-Carotene . . . . **540 mcg**
Lutein & Zeaxanthin . . . . **211 mcg**
Lycopene . . . . **12 mcg**

BROCCOLI AND SHRIMP SAUTÉED WITH CHILI FLAKES & SHREDDED COCONUT

4 SERVINGS • PREPARATION: 10 MINUTES • COOKING: 15 MINUTES • MEDIUM

Broccoli is a perfect vegetable to sauté with just about any meat or seafood, and shrimp makes for the perfect pairing here. Plus, shrimp are a great source of Omega-3s and even contain some vitamin D and B12. It is actually an old wives' tale that they are high in cholesterol, so you need not worry. This delicious recipe is quite easy to prepare after the first time and it is one of the most frequent requests from our friends.

24 large shrimp,
    peeled and deveined

2 cloves garlic

1 tsp. fresh ginger, grated

2 tbsp. lime juice

3 tbsp. olive oil

1½ lbs. broccoli, broken
    into small florets

2 tbsp. shredded coconut

1 tsp. red chili flakes

Salt and pepper to taste

1 In a bowl, mix shrimp, garlic, ginger, lime juice and 2 tbsp. olive oil. Marinate for a few minutes in the refrigerator.

2 Meanwhile, prepare the vegetable steamer bringing water to a boil and steaming the broccoli for 5 minutes.

3 In a large pan on medium to high heat, add 1 tbsp. olive oil and sauté the marinated shrimp for approximately 5 minutes until the shrimp turn pink. Add the broccoli and cook over medium heat for 5 additional minutes.

4 In a small separate pan, mix the shredded coconut with the chili pepper and dry roast a few minutes until golden.

5 Add the dry-roasted mixture to the broccoli and shrimp mixture. Serve immediately.

Nutrition Information

Serving Size **1½ Cups**   Servings **4**

Calories	125	Potassium	654 mg
Calories from fat	38	Total Carbohydrates	18 g
Total Fat	4 g	Dietary Fiber	6 g
Cholesterol	53 mg	Sugars	4 g
Sodium	297 mg	Protein	11 g

Vitamin A	32 %	Folic Acid	30 %
Vitamin C	232 %	Vitamin B12	8 %
Calcium	11 %	Pantothenic Acid	11 %
Iron	9 %	Phosphorus	23 %
Vitamin E	13 %	Magnesium	13 %
Vitamin K	219 %	Zinc	8 %
Vitamin B1	10 %	Selenium	26 %
Vitamin B2	13 %	Copper	10 %
Niacin	10 %	Manganese	26 %
Vitamin B6	18 %		

OTHER BENEFICIAL NUTRIENTS (PER SERVING)

Choline	68 mg
Beta-Carotene	859 mcg
Alpha-Carotene	43 mcg
Lutein & Zeaxanthin	2,533 mcg

BROCCOLI *"SOUFFLÉ"*

6 SERVINGS • PREPARATION: 25 MINUTES • COOKING: 25 MINUTES • DIFFICULT

Broccoli is so remarkably healthy that I am always looking for new and creative ways to make it more enjoyable to eat. Although not a true "soufflé," this little dish is surprisingly rich and filling despite being low in calories and, of course, rich in nutrition. After preparing it once, you will find it much easier to prepare the second time.

1½ lbs. broccoli, broken into florets	⅓ cup garbanzo flour (or corn starch)
3 tbsp. butter	1 cup Swiss cheese, grated
3 eggs, separated	⅛ tsp. nutmeg
¼ cup skim milk	Salt and pepper to taste

1 Preheat oven to 375°. Wash and steam the broccoli for 10 minutes. Reserve a few of the florets for decoration.

2 Blend most of the broccoli in a food processor (or mash with a fork) until smooth.

3 Melt the butter in the microwave for 30 seconds. Pour into a bowl and stir in the egg yolks, milk, garbanzo flour (or corn starch), most of the cheese (reserve some for top), nutmeg, salt and pepper. Reserve.

4 Beat the egg whites with a pinch of salt until fluffy. When you mix the egg whites, be careful not to "brake" them as we say.

5 Mix whites lightly into the broccoli puree and egg yolk mixture.

6 Pour the preparation into 6 soufflé dishes, decorate with a broccoli floret on the top and sprinkle on the rest of the Swiss cheese. Be careful to not fill the soufflé dishes too much because it is going to rise a little bit. Bake for 20 to 25 minutes. Serve warm directly out of the oven.

Nutrition Information

Serving Size **1 Cup**   Servings **6**

Calories	**220**	Potassium	**420 mg**
Calories from fat	**120**	Total Carbohydrates	**16 g**
Total Fat	**13 g**	Dietary Fiber	**3 g**
Cholesterol	**114 mg**	Sugars	**3 g**
Sodium	**159 mg**	Protein	**11 g**

Vitamin A	**23 %**	Vitamin B6	**12 %**
Vitamin C	**153 %**	Folic Acid	**21 %**
Calcium	**22 %**	Vitamin B12	**14 %**
Iron	**7 %**	Pantothenic Acid	**11 %**
Vitamin D3	**7 %**	Phosphorus	**23 %**
Vitamin E	**7 %**	Magnesium	**9 %**
Vitamin K	**145 %**	Zinc	**11 %**
Vitamin B1	**7 %**	Selenium	**19 %**
Vitamin B2	**18 %**	Copper	**4 %**
Niacin	**4 %**	Manganese	**13 %**

OTHER BENEFICIAL NUTRIENTS (PER SERVING)

Choline	**92 mg**
Beta-Carotene	**433 mcg**
Alpha-Carotene	**28 mcg**
Lutein & Zeaxanthin	**1,701 mcg**

ANDREW'S FAVORITE
GRILLED BROCCOLI

6 SERVINGS • PREPARATION: 3 MINUTES • COOKING: 10 MINUTES • VERY EASY

This is Andrew's favorite snack. He says, "It's as good as potato chips…and a whole lot healthier." I make it at least twice a week and it is so easy to prepare that even Andrew will makes it himself in a matter of moments as a snack or side dish. It works well for almost any vegetable you would consider throwing on the grill and best of all, it tastes almost as good when sautéed in a pan.

1 gallon-size Ziploc® bag

1½ lbs. broccoli,
    broken into small florets

3 tbsp. olive oil

1 tbsp. garlic powder

Salt to taste

1 Preheat the grill on high. Place the individual broccoli florets in the Ziploc bag adding the olive oil, garlic powder and salt. Shake the bag.

2 Reduce heat to medium low and grill the broccoli for 5 minutes on each side. It's ready.

Nutrition Information

Serving Size **1 Cup**   Servings **6**

Calories	**84**	Potassium	**377 mg**
Calories from fat	**44**	Total Carbohydrates	**9 g**
Total Fat	**5 g**	Dietary Fiber	**3 g**
Cholesterol	**0 mg**	Sugars	**2 g**
Sodium	**38 mg**	Protein	**3 g**

Vitamin A	**14 %**	Vitamin B6	**11 %**
Vitamin C	**150 %**	Folic Acid	**18 %**
Calcium	**5 %**	Pantothenic Acid	**7 %**
Iron	**5 %**	Phosphorus	**8 %**
Vitamin E	**8 %**	Magnesium	**6 %**
Vitamin K	**147 %**	Zinc	**3 %**
Vitamin B1	**6 %**	Selenium	**5 %**
Vitamin B2	**8 %**	Copper	**3 %**
Niacin	**4 %**	Manganese	**13 %**

OTHER BENEFICIAL NUTRIENTS (PER SERVING)

Choline	**22 mg**
Beta-Carotene	**409 mcg**
Alpha-Carotene	**28 mcg**
Lutein & Zeaxanthin	**1,590 mcg**

BROCCOLINI AND GREEN BEAN
LETTUCE CUPS

4 SERVINGS • PREPARATION: 15 MINUTES • COOKING: 8 MINUTES • EASY

I found a recipe like this in France, but it was very high in calories, since it was made into little pastry pies. I loved the healthy ingredients, so I thought to make it healthier by using lettuce cups instead of the puff pastry. Maybe we're biased, but Andrew and I both thought the healthy version also tasted much better.

1 bunch (1 lb.) Broccolini

1 pack (approx. 1 lb.) green beans

5.5 oz. goat cheese, crumbled

1 head Bibb lettuce

A few sprigs of parsley

For the dressing:

1 tbsp. balsamic vinegar

1 tsp. Dijon mustard

2 tbsp. olive oil

1 small shallot, finely chopped

Salt and pepper to taste

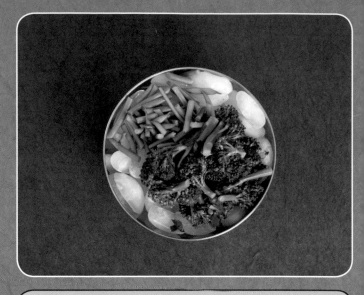

1 Separate the Broccolini into small, bite-sized florets. Cut the ends off the green beans and discard. Then cut green beans into 1"- 2" pieces. Use a steamer basket to steam the Broccolini and green beans for 5 to 8 minutes until bright green and tender.

2 Quickly place the vegetables in a bowl with ice to keep them fresh and brightly colored. Once cool, drain vegetables and pat dry.

3 Wash the Bibb lettuce and remove about eight leaves. Set them on the serving dish.

4 Prepare the dressing: In a bowl, combine the Balsamic vinegar, Dijon mustard, olive oil, chopped shallots, and salt and pepper.

5 In a large bowl mix together the cooked Brocolini, cooked green beans and the crumbled goat cheese with the dressing.

6 Spoon mixture into the lettuce cups and garnish with parsley. Serve immediately.

Nutrition Information

Serving Size **2 Lettuce Cups**   Servings **4**

Calories	**282**	Potassium	**757 mg**
Calories from fat	**173**	Total Carbohydrates	**18 g**
Total Fat	**19 g**	Dietary Fiber	**6 g**
Cholesterol	**31 mg**	Sugars	**7 g**
Sodium	**262 mg**	Protein	**14 g**

Vitamin A	**68 %**	Vitamin B6	**12 %**
Vitamin C	**180 %**	Folic Acid	**35 %**
Calcium	**23 %**	Vitamin B12	**1 %**
Iron	**18 %**	Pantothenic Acid	**10 %**
Vitamin D3	**2 %**	Phosphorus	**28 %**
Vitamin E	**1 %**	Magnesium	**17 %**
Vitamin K	**237 %**	Zinc	**7 %**
Vitamin B1	**15 %**	Selenium	**8 %**
Vitamin B2	**31 %**	Copper	**18 %**
Niacin	**11 %**	Manganese	**30 %**

OTHER BENEFICIAL NUTRIENTS (PER SERVING)

Choline	**47 mg**
Beta-Carotene	**1,652 mcg**
Alpha-Carotene	**102 mcg**
Lutein & Zeaxanthin	**2,771 mcg**

ANDREW'S FAVORITE GRILLED CAULIFLOWER

4 SERVINGS • PREPARATION: 5 MINUTES • COOKING: 10 MINUTES • EASY

Like the grilled broccoli, grilled cauliflower is one of Andrew's favorite snacks or side dishes. He loves it. Sometimes I cook the cauliflower florets in a hot skillet, which works just as well as the grill — although Andrew does love the crunch and flavor from the grill. This recipe works well for preparing almost any vegetable you'd throw on the grill or into a pan. It is so easy to prepare that even Andrew doesn't hesitate to do it himself.

1 head (1½ lbs.) cauliflower	2 tbsp. garlic powder
1 gallon-size Ziploc® bag	Salt to taste
2 tbsp. olive oil	Juice of 1 lemon

1 Preheat the grill on high. Wash cauliflower and break into florets. Into the ziploc bag add the cauliflower, olive oil, garlic powder, salt and lemon juice.

2 Turn the grill down to medium/low. Grill cauliflower for 5 minutes on one side and then 5 minutes on the other side. Add the lemon juice and serve.

Nutrition Information

Serving Size **1 Cup**		Servings **4**

Calories **101**	Potassium . . . . . . **579 mg**	
Calories from fat **53**	Total Carbohydrates . . . **13 g**	
Total Fat . . . . **6 g**	Dietary Fiber . . . . **2 g**	
Cholesterol . . . . **0 mg**	Sugars . . . . **4 g**	
Sodium . . . . **54 mg**	Protein . . . . **5 g**	

Vitamin C . . . . . . **145 %**	Folic Acid . . . . **25 %**	
Calcium . . . . **4 %**	Pantothenic Acid . . . **12 %**	
Iron . . . . **6 %**	Phosphorus . . . . **10 %**	
Vitamin E . . . . **4 %**	Magnesium . . . . **7 %**	
Vitamin K . . . . **36 %**	Zinc . . . . **4 %**	
Vitamin B1 . . . . **7 %**	Selenium . . . . **3 %**	
Vitamin B2 . . . . **8 %**	Copper . . . . **5 %**	
Niacin . . . . **5 %**	Manganese . . . . **16 %**	
Vitamin B6 . . . . **20 %**		

OTHER BENEFICIAL NUTRIENTS (PER SERVING)
Choline . . . . **79 mg**
Lutein & Zeaxanthin . . . . **4 mcg**

CAULIFLOWER CASSEROLE
DE MA GRAND-MÈRE

6 – 8 CUPS • PREPARATION: 20 MINUTES • COOKING: 15 MINUTES • DIFFICULT

My grandmother used to make this as a special treat for me when I was a child. I loved it then and I love it now. Who knew back then how healthy and nutritious cauliflower was? It is such a pleasure to see Andrew now enjoy my Grand-mère's delicious and nutritious cauliflower casserole.

1 head (1½ lbs.) cauliflower

3 tbsp. butter

¼ cup garbanzo flour
   (or regular flour)

1½ cups warm skim milk

1 cup Swiss cheese

Salt and pepper to taste

1 pinch nutmeg

1 Preheat the oven to 375°. Wash the cauliflower and prepare the florets. Steam for 10 minutes with a little salt. You can also cook them in boiling water, but drain them well.

2 While the cauliflower is cooking, make the Béchamel sauce. In a small saucepan, melt 2 tbsp. butter over medium heat. Add the flour at once, whisking rapidly until the mixture thickens and forms a paste.

3 Reduce to a medium low heat, gradually adding the warm skim milk whisking constantly.

4 The sauce should be thickening. The entire process should take approximately 10 minutes. Salt and pepper to taste.

5 Add half of the Swiss cheese. Mix well.

6 Place the cooked cauliflower in a buttered dish. Pour the sauce over the top and sprinkle with the rest of the Swiss cheese and the nutmeg. Bake for 20 minutes or until golden.

Nutrition Information

Serving Size **1 Cup**   Servings **7**

Calories	131	Potassium	407 mg
Calories from fat	73	Total Carbohydrates	12 g
Total Fat	8 g	Dietary Fiber	2 g
Cholesterol	24 mg	Sugars	5 g
Sodium	110 mg	Protein	9 g

Vitamin A	7 %	Vitamin B6	12 %
Vitamin C	78 %	Folic Acid	15 %
Calcium	21 %	Vitamin B12	13 %
Iron	4 %	Pantothenic Acid	9 %
Vitamin D3	3 %	Phosphorus	20 %
Vitamin E	1 %	Magnesium	13 %
Vitamin K	20 %	Zinc	9 %
Vitamin B1	7 %	Selenium	12 %
Vitamin B2	13 %	Copper	4 %
Niacin	4 %	Manganese	19 %

OTHER BENEFICIAL NUTRIENTS (PER SERVING)

Choline	56 mg
Beta-Carotene	18 mcg
Lutein & Zeaxanthin	14 mcg

ANDREW'S MASHED CAULIFLOWER

6 – 8 CUPS • PREPARATION: 5 MINUTES • COOKING: 15 MINUTES • EASY

Andrew loves his mashed potatoes. At family gatherings he remains the "official mashed potato maker;" but, other than holidays, he does not consume them. He wanted us to find a healthy and nutritious version of mashed potatoes without the high calories, carbs and fat. This recipe is a delicious treat that is exceptionally low in calories and full of protective phytonutrients. You can also add your favorite herbs, spices or condiments to expand the flavor possibilities. Like Andrew, you will be astounded how much you will enjoy this healthy alternative to mashed potatoes.

2 heads (3 lbs.) cauliflower	1½ cups vegetable broth
1 tbsp. butter	Salt and pepper to taste
2 tbsp. almond meal	Sprigs of rosemary for garnish

1 Wash the cauliflower and separate the florets. Steam for 15 minutes.

2 Put the cauliflower in the blender with the butter, almond meal and broth. Mix well until pureed (approximately 2 minutes).

3 Add salt and pepper to taste, and serve in individual bowls decorated with rosemary.

Nutrition Information

Serving Size **1 Cup**   Servings **8**

Calories **78**	Potassium . . . . . . **534 mg**
Calories from fat **33**	Total Carbohydrates . . . **10 g**
Total Fat . . . . **4 g**	Dietary Fiber . . . . **2 g**
Cholesterol . . . . . . **4 mg**	Sugars . . . . **4 g**
Sodium . . . . **240 mg**	Protein . . . . **4 g**

Vitamin A . . . . **1 %**	Vitamin B6 . . . . **16 %**
Vitamin C . . . . . . **137 %**	Folic Acid . . . . **25 %**
Calcium . . . . **5 %**	Pantothenic Acid . . . **12 %**
Iron . . . . **5 %**	Phosphorus . . . . **9 %**
Vitamin E . . . . **5 %**	Magnesium . . . . **9 %**
Vitamin K . . . . . . **33 %**	Zinc . . . . **8 %**
Vitamin B1 . . . . **6 %**	Selenium . . . . **7 %**
Vitamin B2 . . . . **9 %**	Copper . . . . **2 %**
Niacin . . . . **5 %**	Manganese . . . . **4 %**

OTHER BENEFICIAL NUTRIENTS (PER SERVING)

Choline . . . . **6 mg**

Beta-Carotene . . . . **20 mcg**

CAULIFLOWER AND TOMATO CASSEROLE WITH ALMONDS AND PARMESAN

6 CUPS • PREPARATION: 20 MINUTES • COOKING: 25 MINUTES • MEDIUM

This recipe provides another delicious way to enjoy the remarkable health benefits of cauliflower with the added flavor and texture of almonds, yogurt and parmesan cheese. They all combine to make this a particularly rich and filling dish. While the photos show it being made in small casseroles, it can also be made in a single large casserole. For added moisture, you can choose to replace the cherry tomatoes with a can of diced tomatoes.

1 head (1½ lb.) cauliflower

1 lb. cherry tomatoes
    (or canned diced tomatoes)

1 tsp. olive oil (optional)

1 tbsp. chives, finely chopped

Salt and pepper to taste

1½ cups plain yogurt

1 tsp. paprika

½ cup almonds, sliced

¾ cup Parmesan cheese,
    shredded

1 Cut the cauliflower into florets and wash them. Steam for 10 minutes with a little salt.

2 Meanwhile, cut the tomatoes in half (or open the can) and distribute them in ramekins after you put a little olive oil at the bottom (optional). Add the chives, salt and pepper. Mix the yogurt well with a spoon and add it to the tomato mixture, along with the paprika. (I mix the paprika in the yogurt.)

3 Add the cooked cauliflower and sprinkle with sliced almonds and cheese.

4 Bake at 375° for 15 minutes (slightly longer for single casserole dish). It should come out golden and delicious.

Nutrition Information

Serving Size **1 Cup**   Servings **6**

Calories	**166**	Potassium	**688 mg**
Calories from fat	**81**	Total Carbohydrates	**14 g**
Total Fat	**9 g**	Dietary Fiber	**3 g**
Cholesterol	**15 mg**	Sugars	**7 g**
Sodium	**236 mg**	Protein	**10 g**

Vitamin A	**20 %**	Folic Acid	**21 %**
Vitamin C	**109 %**	Vitamin B12	**6 %**
Calcium	**25 %**	Pantothenic Acid	**12 %**
Iron	**7 %**	Phosphorus	**24 %**
Vitamin E	**13 %**	Magnesium	**15 %**
Vitamin K	**32 %**	Zinc	**2 %**
Vitamin B1	**8 %**	Selenium	**10 %**
Vitamin B2	**18 %**	Copper	**7 %**
Niacin	**7 %**	Manganese	**14 %**
Vitamin B6	**16 %**		

OTHER BENEFICIAL NUTRIENTS (PER SERVING)

Choline	**23 mg**
Beta-Carotene	**475 mcg**
Alpha-Carotene	**79 mcg**
Lutein & Zeaxanthin	**167 mcg**
Lycopene	**1,947 mcg**

EGG-WHITE FRITTATA WITH COLLARD GREENS, ZUCCHINI AND TURMERIC

8 - 10 CUPS • PREPARATION: 15 MINUTES • COOKING: 25 MINUTES • MEDIUM

Collard greens are remarkably nutritious, but can be difficult to prepare and enjoy. This wonderful dish is not only delicious but, high in protein, low in calories and rich in phytonutrients from the collard greens, turmeric and garlic. I start cooking it in a pan and then place it in the oven to finish at about 375°. Andrew will eat it for breakfast or enjoy it as a snack throughout the day. For me, I like to serve it with a simple arugula salad.

4 leaves (4 cups) collard greens	1 cup red onion, chopped	16 oz. carton (2 cups) egg whites [~15 eggs]
2 medium zucchini	1 clove garlic	½ cup Parmesan cheese, shredded
1 cup tofu, cubed	1 tsp. turmeric	
1 tbsp. olive oil	¼ tsp. cayenne pepper	Salt to taste

1   Preheat oven to 375°. Wash collard greens, remove the vein in the middle and chop into small pieces. Wash and peel the zucchini, and cut into small pieces.

2   Sauté the cut tofu in a HOT pan with oil for 5 minutes until the tofu gets some color.

3 In a medium to large non-stick, ovenproof pan, over medium heat, add olive oil and sauté the onion, garlic, collard greens, zucchini, turmeric and cayenne pepper. Cook for 5 minutes. Add the tofu and SLOWLY add the egg whites. Let it cook on low to medium heat for 5 minutes.

4 Add the shredded cheese on the top and bake for 10 to 15 minutes until golden. Serve warm. You may also refrigerate and serve later.

Nutrition Information

Serving Size **1 Cup**   Servings **10**

Calories	**95**	Potassium	**273 mg**
Calories from fat	**37**	Total Carbohydrates	**5 g**
Total Fat	**4 g**	Dietary Fiber	**1 g**
Cholesterol	**4 mg**	Sugars	**2 g**
Sodium	**190 mg**	Protein	**11 g**

Vitamin A	**15 %**	Folic Acid	**8 %**
Vitamin C	**21 %**	Vitamin B12	**2 %**
Calcium	**20 %**	Pantothenic Acid	**3 %**
Iron	**10 %**	Phosphorus	**10 %**
Vitamin E	**2 %**	Magnesium	**7 %**
Vitamin K	**63 %**	Zinc	**4 %**
Vitamin B1	**4 %**	Selenium	**20 %**
Vitamin B2	**18 %**	Copper	**5 %**
Niacin	**2 %**	Manganese	**17 %**
Vitamin B6	**7 %**		

OTHER BENEFICIAL NUTRIENTS (PER SERVING)

Choline	**9 mg**
Beta-Carotene	**399 mcg**
Alpha-Carotene	**2 mcg**
Lutein & Zeaxanthin	**1,328 mcg**

COLLARD GREENS
AND GREEN BEANS À L'ORANGE

8 SERVINGS • PREPARATION: 10 MINUTES • COOKING: 13 MINUTES • MEDIUM

What a nutritious combination. Collard greens, green beans and a hint of orange. It's so low in calories and its bright colors reveal its rich content of protective phytonutrients. Collard greens are one of those green leafy vegetables, like kale and spinach, which should become a staple of the American diet.

2 packed cups collard greens, chopped

1 lb. green beans

1 tbsp. olive oil

1 shallot, chopped

1 clove garlic, minced

1 yellow or orange bell pepper, julienned (sliced very thin)

3 tbsp. orange juice

Zest of 1 orange

1 tbsp. Balsamic vinegar

1 sprig rosemary

Salt and pepper to taste

1 In a steamer basket, bring water to a boil and cook the green beans for 2 to 3 minutes until tender and bright green.

2 In a large skillet, over medium to high heat, add olive oil with the shallots, garlic and peppers. Sauté for 5 minutes until tender and golden.

3 Reduce heat. Add the green beans, collard greens, juice, zest and vinegar. Add a little rosemary for flavor. Cook for 5 minutes. Salt and pepper to taste. Decorate with rosemary.

Nutrition Information

Serving Size **1 Cup**   Servings **8**

Calories **50**	Potassium . . . . . . **218 mg**
Calories from fat **18**	Total Carbohydrates . . . . **7 g**
Total Fat . . . . **2 g**	Dietary Fiber . . . . **3 g**
Cholesterol . . . . **0 mg**	Sugars . . . . **4 g**
Sodium . . . . **7 mg**	Protein . . . . **2 g**

Vitamin A . . . . **37 %**	Vitamin B6 . . . . **9 %**
Vitamin C . . . . **75 %**	Folic Acid . . . . **12 %**
Calcium . . . . **6 %**	Pantothenic Acid . . . **3 %**
Iron . . . . **4 %**	Phosphorus . . . . **3 %**
Vitamin E . . . . **6 %**	Magnesium . . . . **6 %**
Vitamin K . . . . **90 %**	Zinc . . . . **2 %**
Vitamin B1 . . . . **5 %**	Selenium . . . . **1 %**
Vitamin B2 . . . . **6 %**	Copper . . . . **3 %**
Niacin . . . . **4 %**	Manganese . . . . **13 %**

OTHER BENEFICIAL NUTRIENTS (PER SERVING)

Choline . . . . **14 mg**
Beta-Carotene . . . . **1,017 mcg**
Alpha-Carotene . . . . **46 mcg**
Lutein & Zeaxanthin . . . . **993 mcg**

WASABI-WATERCRESS "NUTTY HUMMUS"

2 CUPS • PREPARATION: 10 MINUTES (PLUS 2 HOURS) • EASY

Hummus is a dip or spread from the Middle East that has been traditionally made from mashed chickpeas (garbanzo beans). Hummus is still one of Andrew's favorite treats but we wanted to have a lower-carb option as well. One day, while experimenting with some cashews I had soaked overnight, we came up with this amazing recipe. It has become one of our favorite dips for veggies or as a spread or sauce. In fact, we use it in our Wasabi Smoked Salmon Green Bean Rolls (Recipe #25). Consuming nuts is a healthy addition to any diet and combined with the health benefits of Wasabi (a cruciferous vegetable) and watercress, it is both delicious and highly nutritious.

1½ cups raw, unsalted cashews, soaked (2 hours min.)

½ to ¾ cup water

2 tbsp. wasabi (to taste)

1 tbsp. olive oil

2 cloves garlic

3 or 4 watercress leaves

1 tbsp. Tahini

Salt and pepper to taste

1 oz. fresh mint

1 tsp. lemon juice (optional)

Selection of favorite veggies for dipping

1 Soak cashews in water for at least 2 hours or overnight. Drain the cashews. Place the cashews into the blender.

2 Add ½ cup of water, wasabi, olive oil, garlic, 3 or 4 leaves of watercress, tahini, mint, lemon juice, salt and pepper (to taste) into the blender. Blend approximately 3 minutes or until smooth. Add more water if necessary to obtain a smooth paste.

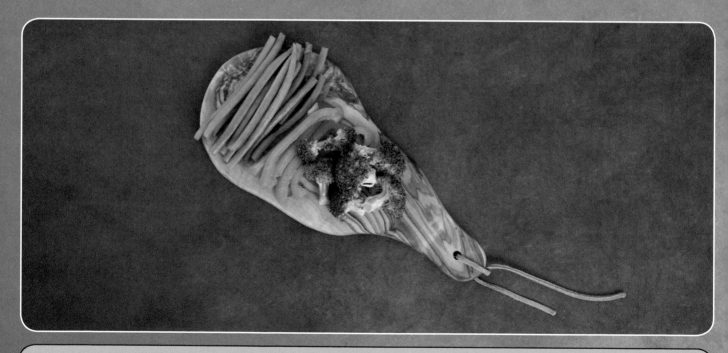

4 Julienne (thinly slice) your selection of vegetables. I like to use steamed green beans, broccoli, cauliflower or bell peppers.

4 Serve with the julienned vegetables. You may also serve with pita bread or crackers.

Nutrition Information

Serving Size **1 tsp.**   Servings **32**

Calories	38	Potassium	38 mg
Calories from fat	28	Total Carbohydrates	2 g
Total Fat	3 g	Dietary Fiber	0 g
Cholesterol	0 mg	Sugars	0 g
Sodium	2 mg	Protein	1 g

Vitamin C	1 %	Folic Acid	1 %
Calcium	1 %	Pantothenic Acid	1 %
Iron	2 %	Phosphorus	3 %
Vitamin E	1 %	Magnesium	4 %
Vitamin K	3 %	Zinc	2 %
Vitamin B1	1 %	Selenium	1 %
Vitamin B2	1 %	Copper	6 %
Niacin	1 %	Manganese	2 %
Vitamin B6	1 %		

OTHER BENEFICIAL NUTRIENTS (PER SERVING)

Choline	3 mg
Beta-Carotene	6 mcg
Lutein & Zeaxanthin	19 mcg

WASABI SMOKED SALMON GREEN BEAN ROLLS

8 ROLLS • PREPARATION: 15 MINUTES • COOKING: 5 MINUTES • MEDIUM

Salmon is the fish we consume most at home and we are always looking for ways to "spice it up" just a bit. These little rolls do just that since we serve them with our Wasabi-Watercress "Nutty Hummus" (Recipe #24). That Nutty Sauce gives them quite a "kick". You can also serve them in lettuce or cabbage cups, if you can't find rice or soy paper. If your grocer does not carry them, you can usually find any of the more exotic ingredients from these recipes readily available at numerous websites on-line or at Amazon.com.

1 lb. green beans

8 oz. smoked salmon

8 sheets rice or soy paper

2 oz. sprouts

Wasabi-Watercress *"Nutty Hummus"* (Recipe #24)

1 Cut off the ends of the green beans. In a steamer basket, steam the green beans for 5 minutes until crisp and bright green.

2 Detail the smoked salmon into 8 thin slices.

3 Spread a sheet of rice or soy paper on a damp paper towel. Place the salmon on the paper first, then the hummus, then 4 or 5 green beans and a few of the sprouts, and roll tightly.

4 Cut each roll into 2 or 4 pieces, and serve with additional "*Nutty Hummus*" on the side.

Nutrition Information

Serving Size **1 Cup**   Servings **4**

Calories **105**	Potassium . . . . . . **350 mg**
Calories from fat **25**	Total Carbohydrates . . . . **8 g**
Total Fat . . . . **3 g**	Dietary Fiber . . . . **3 g**
Cholesterol . . . . . . **13 mg**	Sugars . . . . **4 g**
Sodium . . . . **452 mg**	Protein . . . . **13 g**

Vitamin A . . . . **17 %**	Vitamin B6 . . . . **16 %**
Vitamin C . . . . **25 %**	Folic Acid . . . . **11 %**
Calcium . . . . **5 %**	Vitamin B12 . . . . . . **31 %**
Iron . . . . **10 %**	Pantothenic Acid . . . . **8 %**
Vitamin D3 . . . . **97 %**	Phosphorus . . . . . . **15 %**
Vitamin E . . . . **6 %**	Magnesium . . . . **11 %**
Vitamin K . . . . **26 %**	Zinc . . . . **4 %**
Vitamin B1 . . . . **8 %**	Selenium . . . . **27 %**
Vitamin B2 . . . . **11 %**	Copper . . . . **12 %**
Niacin . . . . **18 %**	Manganese . . . . **14 %**

OTHER BENEFICIAL NUTRIENTS (PER SERVING)

Choline	**70 mg**
Beta-Carotene	**442 mcg**
Alpha-Carotene	**79 mcg**
Lutein & Zeaxanthin	**726 mcg**

DICED ASPARAGUS, AVOCADO AND TOMATO TARTAR

6 – 8 CUPS • PREPARATION: 20 MINUTES • COOKING: 7 MINUTES • EASY

This is a simple and easy recipe, since the only cooking required is a light steaming of the asparagus. It is a light, fresh and wonderfully healthy recipe that provides high levels of a long list of essential and protective nutrients. Andrew loves it as a low-calorie but filling snack, or as a perfect light appetizer before a meal.

1 lb. asparagus

1 pinch salt (to taste)

1 lb. cherry tomatoes, quartered

2 ripe avocados, peeled
    and cubed

2 tbsp. olive oil

Juice of 1 lemon

1 tsp. agave or honey

1 oz. tarragon

1 oz. fresh mint

Salt and pepper to taste

¼ tsp. Sriracha or Tabasco®

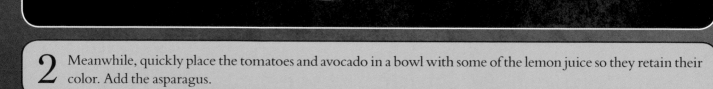

1 Remove the bottom inch of the stem from the asparagus and discard. Cut the rest into small pieces including the head. Steam for 5 to 7 minutes with a little salt. (Cooking time depends on the thickness of the asparagus.) I like to keep them crunchy.

2 Meanwhile, quickly place the tomatoes and avocado in a bowl with some of the lemon juice so they retain their color. Add the asparagus.

3 Chop the mint and tarragon. Make the dressing by mixing the olive oil, lemon juice, agave, tarragon, mint, and salt and pepper to taste.

4 Add the cooked asparagus to the vegetables in the bowl and stir in the dressing. Add the Sriracha or Tabasco. Mix well and decorate with some mint or tarragon leaves. I like to serve in martini glasses to show off the beautiful colors.

Nutrition Information

Serving Size **1 Cup**   Servings **8**

Calories	**146**	Potassium	**605 mg**
Calories from fat	**101**	Total Carbohydrates	**12 g**
Total Fat	**11 g**	Dietary Fiber	**6 g**
Cholesterol	**0 mg**	Sugars	**4 g**
Sodium	**10 mg**	Protein	**4 g**

Vitamin A	**22 %**	Vitamin B6	**16 %**
Vitamin C	**33 %**	Folic Acid	**22 %**
Calcium	**7 %**	Pantothenic Acid	**9 %**
Iron	**16 %**	Phosphorus	**8 %**
Vitamin E	**2 %**	Magnesium	**10 %**
Vitamin K	**51 %**	Zinc	**6 %**
Vitamin B1	**10 %**	Selenium	**2 %**
Vitamin B2	**12 %**	Copper	**13 %**
Niacin	**10 %**	Manganese	**25 %**

OTHER BENEFICIAL NUTRIENTS (PER SERVING)

Choline	**20 mg**
Beta-Carotene	**541 mcg**
Alpha-Carotene	**75 mcg**
Lutein & Zeaxanthin	**610 mcg**
Lycopene	**1,460 mcg**

ASPARAGUS BUNDLES IN PROSCIUTTO WITH PARMESAN

4 SERVINGS • PREPARATION: 10 MINUTES • COOKING: 10 MINUTES • EASY

A quick and easy recipe to prepare, the brief cooking time depends on the thickness of the asparagus spears. I prefer using three spears per bundle and two bundles are more than enough for a perfectly healthy appetizer or side dish. Andrew finds that the prosciutto and parmesan provide a deliciously classic Italian flavor to the incomparable nutrition of asparagus.

Olive oil spray

2 bunches (1½ lbs.) asparagus

5 oz. prosciutto or pancetta

Salt and pepper to taste

½ cup Parmesan cheese, shredded

1 Lightly spray baking sheet with olive oil (I cover the sheet with tin foil to minimize cleanup). Wash and trim asparagus. Cut prosciutto in half lengthwise and wrap around 3 asparagus, placing bundles on baking sheet. Salt and pepper, and sprinkle with Parmesan cheese.

2 Place under a LIGHT broiler for 5 minutes until crispy. Turn over with tongs and cook for 5 additional minutes.

3 Serve warm as an appetizer or side dish.

Nutrition Information

Serving Size **1 Bundle**   Servings **4**

Calories **143**	Potassium . . . . . **455 mg**	
Calories from fat **64**	Total Carbohydrates . . . . **8 g**	
Total Fat . . . . **7 g**	Dietary Fiber . . . . **4 g**	
Cholesterol . . . **27 mg**	Sugars . . . . **3 g**	
Sodium . . . . **636 mg**	Protein . . . . **8 g**	

Vitamin A . . . . **27 %**	Folic Acid. . . . . **23 %**	
Vitamin C . . . . **18 %**	Vitamin B12 . . . . **5 %**	
Calcium . . . . **17 %**	Pantothenic Acid . . . . **7 %**	
Iron . . . . **23 %**	Phosphorus. . . . . . . **22 %**	
Vitamin E. . . . . . . **11 %**	Magnesium. . . . . **9 %**	
Vitamin K . . . . . . **90 %**	Zinc . . . . **11 %**	
Vitamin B1 . . . . . . **31 %**	Selenium . . . . **19 %**	
Vitamin B2 . . . . . . **20 %**	Copper. . . . . **18 %**	
Niacin . . . . **14 %**	Manganese . . . . . . **23 %**	
Vitamin B6 . . . . . . **14 %**		

OTHER BENEFICIAL NUTRIENTS (PER SERVING)

Choline.	**58 mg**
Beta–Carotene.	**770 mcg**
Alpha–Carotene	**15 mcg**
Lutein & Zeaxanthin.	**1,207 mcg**

ASPARAGUS, SALMON AND BABY CORN ASIAN SAUTÉ

6 CUPS • PREPARATION: 10 MINUTES • COOKING: 10 MINUTES • MEDIUM

I often hear that grilled, broiled or baked salmon can get a little boring and this easy-to-prepare recipe gives a delicious Asian flair to our favorite healthy fish. My greatest challenge with this recipe is adding the baby corn before Andrew eats them separately. He loves them. This recipe is high in protein, omega-3s and vitamins, yet low in calories. Best of all, you will likely find many other uses for the delicious, low-calorie Asian sauce that we created here.

1 lb. asparagus

1 lb. wild salmon,
    boneless and skinless

1 tsp. canola oil

1 tsp. dark sesame oil

1 tsp. agave

3 garlic cloves, minced

1 tsp. red chili pepper flakes

2 tbsp. low-sodium soy sauce

1 tsp. minced ginger

2 tbsp. mirin
    (Japanese rice wine)

1 tsp. cornstarch

7 oz. jar baby corn (12 ears)

1 Wash and cut the asparagus into small pieces.

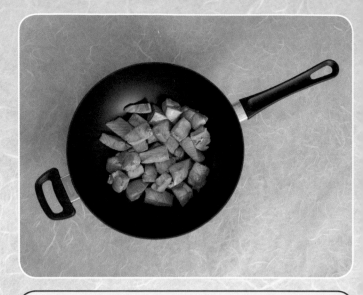

2 Cut the salmon. Over medium heat in a pan or wok, add canola oil and sauté the salmon for 3 minutes. Stir lightly. Reserve on a separate plate.

3 In a bowl, whisk the sesame oil, agave, garlic, chili pepper, soy sauce, ginger, mirin and cornstarch.

4 Add the asparagus to the wok and sauté for 3 minutes.

5 Add the sauce mixture, baby corn and salmon. Cook everything together for 3 to 4 minutes. Serve warm.

Nutrition Information

Serving Size **1 Cup**		Servings **6**

Calories **142**	Potassium . . . . . . **481 mg**
Calories from fat **58**	Total Carbohydrates . . . . **4 g**
Total Fat . . . . **6 g**	Dietary Fiber . . . . **1 g**
Cholesterol . . . . . . **42 mg**	Sugars . . . . **2 g**
Sodium . . . . **213 mg**	Protein . . . . **16 g**

Vitamin A . . . . **13 %**	Folic Acid. . . . . **10 %**
Vitamin C . . . . **5 %**	Vitamin B12 . . . . . . **40 %**
Calcium . . . . **2 %**	Pantothenic Acid . . . **14 %**
Iron . . . . **9 %**	Phosphorus . . . . **18 %**
Vitamin E . . . . **4 %**	Magnesium. . . . . **8 %**
Vitamin K . . . . **21 %**	Zinc . . . . **5 %**
Vitamin B1 . . . . . . **16 %**	Selenium . . . . **41 %**
Vitamin B2 . . . . **21 %**	Copper . . . . **14 %**
Niacin . . . . **33 %**	Manganese . . . . **7 %**
Vitamin B6 . . . . . . **35 %**	

OTHER BENEFICIAL NUTRIENTS (PER SERVING)	
Omega-3 (ALA) . . . . **1 mg**
Choline. . . . . **9 mg**
Beta-Carotene. . . . . **334 mcg**
Alpha-Carotene . . . . **4 mcg**
Lutein & Zeaxanthin. . . . . **368 mcg**

SAUTÉED ASPARAGUS TO "BRAGG" ABOUT

4 SERVINGS • PREPARATION: 5 MINUTES • COOKING: 10 MINUTES • VERY EASY

Our friends, Hal and Greg, shared this delicious and simple recipe that can also be used to sauté a myriad of other healthy vegetables. It makes a veggie snack or side dish delicious, nutritious and extremely low in calories. For many, the best part of this recipe will be the discovery of Bragg® Liquid Aminos — a seasoning invented decades ago by Paul Bragg, one of America's original health pioneers. Andrew has used Bragg Liquid Aminos as a healthy condiment for more than 30 years. Often, rather than a sauté, I will grill the asparagus or other healthy vegetable, since Andrew loves the resulting crunchy texture and grilled flavor.

1 lb. asparagus, with ends
  removed

2 tbsp. olive oil

1 tbsp. Bragg® Liquid Aminos
  (or low-sodium soy sauce)

1 tbsp. garlic powder

1 tsp. crushed pepper

1 gallon-size Ziploc® bag

1 Place the asparagus in the Ziploc bag along with olive oil, Bragg, garlic powder and crushed pepper. Shake the bag gently.

2 In a warm pan or on the grill, cook the asparagus for approximately 5 minutes on each side. They should be bright green and a little crunchy.

Nutrition Information

Serving Size **6 Asparagus**   Servings **4**

Calories **77**	Potassium . . . . . . **289 mg**
Calories from fat **44**	Total Carbohydrates . . . . **7 g**
Total Fat . . . . **5 g**	Dietary Fiber . . . . **3 g**
Cholesterol . . . . **0 mg**	Sugars . . . . **2 g**
Sodium . . . . **154 mg**	Protein . . . . **3 g**

Vitamin A . . . . **27 %**	Vitamin B6 . . . . **9 %**
Vitamin C . . . . **12 %**	Folic Acid . . . . **16 %**
Calcium . . . . **3 %**	Pantothenic Acid . . . . **3 %**
Iron . . . . **15 %**	Phosphorus . . . . **8 %**
Vitamin E . . . . **11 %**	Magnesium . . . . **5 %**
Vitamin K . . . . **62 %**	Zinc . . . . **5 %**
Vitamin B1 . . . . **12 %**	Selenium . . . . **5 %**
Vitamin B2 . . . . **11 %**	Copper . . . . **12 %**
Niacin . . . . **7 %**	Manganese . . . . **12 %**

OTHER BENEFICIAL NUTRIENTS (PER SERVING)

Choline	**22 mg**
Beta-Carotene	**755 mcg**
Alpha-Carotene	**10 mcg**
Lutein & Zeaxanthin	**954 mcg**

VERY GREEN ASPARAGUS RISOTTO

7 – 8 CUPS • PREPARATION: 15 MINUTES • COOKING: 35 TO 40 MINUTES • DIFFICULT

Andrew reluctantly allowed me to include this recipe, since although he loves the taste of risotto or even brown rice, he rarely consumes them given their high carbohydrate and caloric content. Brown rice is a slightly more nutritious choice here, but Andrew still insists that I reduce the rice and increase the asparagus when we make it at home. You can do the same, but don't forget that brown rice generally takes a bit longer to prepare. Andrew also ensures that, despite how delicious this is, or precisely because it is so delicious, we pay careful attention to portion size.

For the risotto:

1 tbsp. olive oil

1 medium red onion, chopped

1 garlic clove

1 cup Arborio rice

½ cup white wine

4 cups warm vegetable broth
   or water

1 lb. asparagus, cut into small
   pieces

½ cup Parmesan cheese, shredded

For the pesto:

1 pack (1 oz.) basil

½ cup pine nuts

2 garlic cloves

1 tbsp. olive oil

1 In a large skillet, add 1 tbsp. olive oil, chopped onion, one garlic clove and the Arborio rice. Sauté over medium heat until the rice becomes translucent – approximately 5 minutes. Reduce heat, add the wine and mix well. Cook for an additional 5 minutes until the wine is absorbed.

2 Meanwhile, in a mini food processor (or hand chop very finely) add the basil, pine nuts, one garlic clove and 1 tbsp. olive oil, blending until you obtain a green paste (Pesto). Reserve.

3 Add a cup of broth to the rice. Let the rice absorb the broth (approximately 5 minutes). Add remaing cups of broth, one cup at a time, waiting each time for the rice to absorb the liquid. At this point your rice will have cooked for approximately 20 minutes and should be tender, not sticky.

4 Add the asparagus to the rice. Continue to cook for approximately 5 to 7 minutes, less if the asparagus spears are thin.

5 Add the Pesto and Parmesan cheese. Mix all together. Serve right away. It's amazing and it's a meal.

Nutrition Information

Serving Size **1 Cup**   Servings **8**

Calories	**217**	Potassium	**298 mg**
Calories from fat	**87**	Total Carbohydrates	**25 g**
Total Fat	**10 g**	Dietary Fiber	**3 g**
Cholesterol	**4 mg**	Sugars	**3 g**
Sodium	**560 mg**	Protein	**7 g**

Vitamin A	**29 %**	Folic Acid	**12 %**
Vitamin C	**11 %**	Vitamin B12	**1 %**
Calcium	**11 %**	Pantothenic Acid	**6 %**
Iron	**15 %**	Phosphorus	**21 %**
Vitamin E	**10 %**	Magnesium	**19 %**
Vitamin K	**110 %**	Zinc	**11 %**
Vitamin B1	**15 %**	Selenium	**12 %**
Vitamin B2	**9 %**	Copper	**17 %**
Niacin	**11 %**	Manganese	**95 %**
Vitamin B6	**12 %**		

OTHER BENEFICIAL NUTRIENTS (PER SERVING)

Choline	**25 mg**
Beta-Carotene	**704 mcg**
Alpha-Carotene	**5 mcg**
Lutein & Zeaxanthin	**1,202 mcg**

SWISS CHARD WITH SHIITAKE MUSHROOM

4 – 6 CUPS • PREPARATION: 10 MINUTES • COOKING: 10 MINUTES • EASY

The Asian mushrooms are full of phytonutrients and make a wonderful combination with healthy Swiss chard. This side dish makes any meal a remarkably healthy and nutritious experience. I have also made this with standard mushrooms when shiitakes were not available and it is just as tasty. At home, I often add a tablespoon of heavy cream to make it just a little bit richer and Andrew loves the rich, filling flavor and the fact that it is still very low in calories.

4 cups (~7 oz) Rainbow Swiss chard, finely minced	1 tbsp. olive oil	½ cup parsley, chopped
28 oz. Shiitake mushrooms, sliced	1 shallot, minced	Salt and pepper to taste
	2 cloves garlic, minced	1 – 2 tbsp. heavy cream (optional)

1 In a large skillet over medium heat, add olive oil and sauté the shallots, garlic and mushrooms for about 3 minutes.

2 Add the chard and sauté for about 5 minutes until the greens are bright colored and tender. Add the parsley and season with salt and pepper. Cook for 2 more minutes, adding heavy cream if you like.

3 Serve warm as a side dish.

Nutrition Information

Serving Size **1 Cup**   Servings **4**

Calories **53**	Potassium . . . . . . **364 mg**
Calories from fat **24**	Total Carbohydrates . . . . **7 g**
Total Fat . . . . **3 g**	Dietary Fiber . . . . **2 g**
Cholesterol . . . . **0 mg**	Sugars . . . . **2 g**
Sodium . . . . **86 mg**	Protein . . . . **3 g**

Vitamin A . . . . **57 %**	Vitamin B6 . . . . . . **12 %**
Vitamin C . . . . **36 %**	Folic Acid . . . . **6 %**
Calcium . . . . **3 %**	Pantothenic Acid . . . . **9 %**
Iron . . . . **8 %**	Phosphorus . . . . **9 %**
Vitamin D3 . . . . **3 %**	Magnesium . . . . **11 %**
Vitamin E . . . . **5 %**	Zinc . . . . **5 %**
Vitamin K . . . . . . **529 %**	Selenium . . . . **5 %**
Vitamin B1 . . . . **2 %**	Copper . . . . **8 %**
Vitamin B2 . . . . **10 %**	Manganese . . . . **15 %**
Niacin . . . . **12 %**	

OTHER BENEFICIAL NUTRIENTS (PER SERVING)

Choline . . . . **7 mg**
Beta-Carotene . . . . **1,313 mcg**
Alpha-Carotene . . . . **16 mcg**
Lutein & Zeaxanthin . . . . **3,960 mcg**

RAINBOW SWISS CHARD
SAUTÉED WITH PINE NUTS AND DRIED APRICOTS

4 - 6 CUPS • PREPARATION: 10 MINUTES • COOKING: 7 MINUTES • EASY

Andrew and I try to eat leafy greens every day and this is a simple way to do so. It is now well-established that leafy greens are among the healthiest foods and Swiss chard is at the top of the list along with Spinach and Kale. Surprisingly, Swiss chard is closely related to the beet, but unlike the beet, concentrates its nutrition in its leaves. The rich colors of rainbow chard are not just beautiful, but indicative of its abundant phytonutrient content. I cook all my greens only as much as required in order to maximize their nutrient content. This dish can also be made with dried cranberries instead of apricots, or even fresh nectarines in season.

4 cups (~7 oz) Rainbow Swiss chard, finely minced

½ medium red onion

2 tbsp. olive oil

2 cloves garlic, minced

¾ cup dried apricots or cranberries

½ cup pine nuts

1 tsp. lemon juice (optional)

Salt and pepper to taste

1 Wash the chard removing the stem and cutting in very thin slices. Chop the onion.

2 In a warm pan over medium heat, add the olive oil, chard, garlic and onion, and sauté for 3 minutes or until the leaves are tender.

3 Add the dried apricots and pine nuts, and sauté 2 additional minutes. Add the lemon juice and mix well. Serve right away with salt and pepper, if you like.

Nutrition Information

Serving Size **1 Cup**   Servings **6**

Calories	**139**	Potassium	**456 mg**
Calories from fat	**99**	Total Carbohydrates	**10 g**
Total Fat	**11 g**	Dietary Fiber	**2 g**
Cholesterol	**0 mg**	Sugars	**6 g**
Sodium	**163 mg**	Protein	**3 g**

Vitamin A	**98 %**	Vitamin B6	**6 %**
Vitamin C	**40 %**	Folic Acid	**4 %**
Calcium	**5 %**	Pantothenic Acid	**2 %**
Iron	**12 %**	Phosphorus	**11 %**
Vitamin E	**16 %**	Magnesium	**23 %**
Vitamin K	**795 %**	Zinc	**7 %**
Vitamin B1	**5 %**	Selenium	**2 %**
Vitamin B2	**6 %**	Copper	**6 %**
Niacin	**5 %**	Manganese	**66 %**

OTHER BENEFICIAL NUTRIENTS (PER SERVING)

Choline	**22 mg**
Beta-Carotene	**2,918 mcg**
Alpha-Carotene	**34 mcg**
Lutein & Zeaxanthin	**8,325 mcg**

SWISS CHARD EGG-WHITE FRITTATA DE PROVENCE WITH FETA CHEESE

8 - 10 CUPS • PREPARATION: 10 MINUTES • COOKING: 28 MINUTES • MEDIUM

This is my French Mediterranean version of a frittata and I love the subtle lavender imparted from the Herbs de Provence. Andrew also loves this tasty treat and will have it for a snack or lunch or even breakfast. He often talks about how healthy Swiss chard is, but like the super-food kale, how little Americans consume of it. Andrew hopes that this book will help us all eat more of these remarkably healthy vegetables.

2 tbsp. olive oil

4 cups (~7 oz) Swiss chard, finely minced

½ medium red onion, chopped

1 clove garlic, minced

Salt and pepper to taste

½ cup feta cheese, crumbled

1 cup cherry tomatoes, halved

2 cups (~15) egg whites

1 tsp. Herbs de Provence with lavender

1 Preheat the oven to 375°. In a medium-size, ovenproof pan over medium heat, add the olive oil, minced chard, onion, garlic, salt and pepper. Sauté for approximately 5 minutes.

2 Add the feta and tomatoes on top of the chard mixture. Slowly add the egg whites. Sprinkle with Herbs de Provence and cook for 3 minutes without touching it. Then, bake 20 minutes at 375°.

3 Serve warm with a side salad (or better yet, some watercress). You may also serve cold, cut as an appetizer.

Nutrition Information

Serving Size 1 Cup   Servings **10**

Calories **69**	Potassium . . . . . . **183 mg**
Calories from fat **32**	Total Carbohydrates . . . . **2 g**
Total Fat . . . . **4 g**	Dietary Fiber . . . . **1 g**
Cholesterol . . . . **0 mg**	Sugars . . . . **1 g**
Sodium . . . . **196 mg**	Protein . . . . **7 g**

Vitamin A . . . . **21 %**	Folic Acid. . . . . **2 %**
Vitamin C . . . . **11 %**	Vitamin B12 . . . . **3 %**
Calcium . . . . **5 %**	Pantothenic Acid . . . . **2 %**
Iron . . . . **2 %**	Phosphorus. . . . . **4 %**
Vitamin E. . . . . **3 %**	Magnesium. . . . . **5 %**
Vitamin K . . . . **152 %**	Zinc . . . . **2 %**
Vitamin B1 . . . . **2 %**	Selenium . . . . **16 %**
Vitamin B2. . . . . . . **17 %**	Copper . . . . **3 %**
Niacin . . . . **1 %**	Manganese . . . . **4 %**
Vitamin B6 . . . . **4 %**	

OTHER BENEFICIAL NUTRIENTS (PER SERVING)

Choline.	**6 mg**
Beta-Carotene.	**592 mcg**
Alpha-Carotene	**22 mcg**
Lutein & Zeaxanthin.	**1,603 mcg**
Lycopene.	**383 mcg**

Swiss Chard Casserole with Quinoa and Tomatoes

8 – 10 CUPS • PREPARATION: 15 MINUTES • COOKING: 30 MINUTES • MEDIUM

Since Andrew and I do not eat rice, pasta, potatoes or bread at home, we are always seeking healthier, nutrient-rich alternatives. Most folks mistakenly consider quinoa a grain, but Andrew assures me that it is absolutely not a grain. In fact, the quinoa seed is surprisingly most closely related to spinach, beets or even Swiss chard. How technically appropriate then to combine the rich nutrition and health benefits of Swiss chard with its nutritious close relative - quinoa.

1 cup quinoa (yellow or red)

4 cups (~7 oz) Rainbow Swiss chard, finely minced

3 cups vegetable broth or water

1 can (14.5 oz.) diced tomatoes

2 tbsp. olive oil

1 small, red onion, chopped

Salt and pepper to taste

¾ cup mozzarella cheese, shredded

1 Preheat the oven to 375°. Cook the quinoa according to the box instructions, usually 1 cup of uncooked quinoa in 2 cups of broth or water in a saucepan. Bring to a boil. Reduce heat and cover. Simmer for 15 minutes depending on the kind of quinoa you are using. (I like the red kind.)

2 While the quinoa is cooking, chop the chard and open the can of diced tomatoes.

3 In a skillet over medium heat, add 1 tbsp. of the olive oil and sauté the chard and onion for 5 minutes.

4 Add the tomatoes, remaining broth (maybe a little less than a cup), the quinoa, and salt and pepper. Cook everything together for 2 minutes over medium to high heat.

5 Prepare the casserole dish by adding remaining olive oil to the bottom of the dish and spreading it with your fingers. Add the quinoa and chard mixture, and cover with the mozzarella cheese. Bake for 15 minutes until golden.

Nutrition Information

Serving Size **1 Cup**		Servings **8**

Calories **154**		Potassium . . . . . . **376 mg**	
Calories from fat **55**		Total Carbohydrates . . . **19 g**	
Total Fat . . . . **6 g**		Dietary Fiber . . . . **7 g**	
Cholesterol . . . . **8 mg**		Sugars . . . . **3 g**	
Sodium . . . . **483 mg**		Protein . . . . **6 g**	

Vitamin A . . . . **48 %**		Folic Acid. . . . . **14 %**	
Vitamin C . . . . **27 %**		Vitamin B12. . . . . **4 %**	
Calcium . . . . **9 %**		Pantothenic Acid. . . . **3 %**	
Iron . . . . **9 %**		Phosphorus. . . . . . . **16 %**	
Vitamin E. . . . . **8 %**		Magnesium. . . . . . . **18 %**	
Vitamin K . . . . . **301 %**		Zinc . . . . **8 %**	
Vitamin B1. . . . . **8 %**		Selenium . . . . **6 %**	
Vitamin B2. . . . .**8 %**		Copper. . . . . **11 %**	
Niacin . . . . **4 %**		Manganese . . . . **31 %**	
Vitamin B6. . . . . . **10 %**			

OTHER BENEFICIAL NUTRIENTS (PER SERVING)

Choline. . . . . **26 mg**	
Beta-Carotene. . . . . **1,271 mcg**	
Alpha-Carotene . . . . **64 mcg**	
Lutein & Zeaxanthin. . . . . **3,219 mcg**	
Lycopene. **1,306 mcg**	

ZUCCHINI CASSEROLE WITH ALMONDS AND PARMESAN CHEESE

8 CUPS • PREPARATION: 20 MINUTES • COOKING: 35 MINUTES • DIFFICULT

This recipe can be a little time consuming, but it is truly worth it. I enjoy the taste and texture combination of zucchini with almonds, parmesan cheese and a little nutmeg. It makes a great snack, light meal, or side dish. Zucchini is low in calories and so versatile; it blends well with other flavors and the results are always delicious and nutritious. If you cannot find almond meal at your local grocery store or gourmet shop, then you can always grind some almonds or, easiest of all, order it on the internet.

2 lbs. zucchini	¼ cup skim milk	Salt and pepper to taste
1 tbsp. olive oil	3 tbsp. almond meal	1 tsp. nutmeg
1 pinch salt	½ cup Parmesan cheese, shredded	¼ cup almonds, sliced
3 eggs		

1 Preheat the oven to 375°. Peel the zucchini and cut into thin slices.

2 In a skillet over medium heat, sauté the zucchini for 5 minutes with half of the olive oil and a little salt. Reserve.

3 In a medium sized bowl, beat the eggs with the skim milk, almond meal, and Parmesan cheese. Salt and pepper to taste.

4 Prepare a baking dish by spreading the remaining olive oil on the bottom and placing the zucchini in the dish. Sprinkle nutmeg on the top.

5 Cover with the egg mixture. Sprinkle the sliced almonds. Bake for 30 minutes. Serve hot.

Nutrition Information

Serving Size **1 Cup**   Servings **8**

Calories	93	Potassium	356 mg
Calories from fat	53	Total Carbohydrates	5 g
Total Fat	6 g	Dietary Fiber	1 g
Cholesterol	65 mg	Sugars	3 g
Sodium	121 mg	Protein	6 g

Vitamin A	7 %	Vitamin B6	11 %
Vitamin C	34 %	Folic Acid	9 %
Calcium	11 %	Vitamin B12	4 %
Iron	5 %	Pantothenic Acid	6 %
Vitamin D3	4 %	Phosphorus	13 %
Vitamin E	6 %	Magnesium	9 %
Vitamin K	7 %	Zinc	6 %
Vitamin B1	5 %	Selenium	10 %
Vitamin B2	14 %	Copper	5 %
Niacin	3 %	Manganese	14 %

OTHER BENEFICIAL NUTRIENTS (PER SERVING)

Choline	63 mg
Beta-Carotene	140 mcg
Lutein & Zeaxanthin	2,495 mcg

STUFFED BELL PEPPERS WITH MILLET, MUSHROOMS AND TURMERIC

6 SERVINGS • PREPARATION: 30 MINUTES • COOKING: 35 MINUTES • DIFFICULT

The colorful bell peppers have become one of the staples in our kitchen. In this recipe we stuff them with millet - an unusual ingredient here in America, but very common throughout Asia and Africa. Millet grows well in arid environments and it is among the world's oldest cultivated foods dating back more than 10,000 years. It is remarkably high in protein and fiber, as well as many other vitamins and minerals. Millet does take some time to cook, so begin cooking it first on the stove and it will be done by the time you have prepared the peppers and cooked the other ingredients.

1 cup millet (or brown rice)	3 cloves garlic	½ cup pine nuts
2 cups water	1 tbsp. olive oil	½ cup chicken or vegetable broth
1 pinch salt (optional)	1 tbsp. turmeric	
6 yellow, orange or red peppers	1 tsp. cumin	Salt and pepper to taste
1 small red onion	1 cup mushrooms, diced	3 tbsp. fresh parsley for garnish

1 Preheat the oven to 375°. Cook the millet according to the box instructions, which is usually 1 cup of millet for 2 cups water with a little salt. Bring to a boil. Cover and reduce heat. Simmer for 20 minutes. Reserve.

2 While the millet is cooking, remove the top of the bell peppers to make a little hat. Remove the seeds, core and place peppers in a baking dish. Chop the onion and mince the garlic.

3 In a medium to large skillet, over medium heat, add the olive oil, garlic, onion, turmeric, cumin, mushrooms and pine nuts. Cook for 10 minutes.

4 Add the cooked millet to the skillet along with the broth (add more broth, if needed) and cook for 5 more minutes. Salt and pepper to taste.

5 Stuff the peppers with the skillet mixture and bake for 25 minutes until the skin darkens. Garnish with parsley. We prefer to cut the peppers in half to double the servings.

Nutrition Information

Serving Size **1 Pepper**   Servings **6**

Calories	290	Potassium	638 mg
Calories from fat	108	Total Carbohydrates	41 g
Total Fat	12 g	Dietary Fiber	6 g
Cholesterol	0 mg	Sugars	1 g
Sodium	76 mg	Protein	8 g

Vitamin A	11 %	Vitamin B6	27 %
Vitamin C	15 %	Folic Acid	22 %
Calcium	4 %	Pantothenic Acid	8 %
Iron	19 %	Phosphorus	23 %
Vitamin E	7 %	Magnesium	24 %
Vitamin K	49 %	Zinc	12 %
Vitamin B1	17 %	Selenium	5 %
Vitamin B2	13 %	Copper	33 %
Niacin	21 %	Manganese	96 %

OTHER BENEFICIAL NUTRIENTS (PER SERVING)

Choline	10 mg
Beta-Carotene	228 mcg
Lutein & Zeaxanthin	4 mcg

ROASTED BELL PEPPERS WITH OLIVES

4 SERVINGS • PREPARATION: 15 MINUTES • COOKING: 15 MINUTES • VERY EASY

This recipe is simple and easy and always a success. My food choices have always been influenced by the healthy Mediterranean diet and this dish is about as "Mediterranean" as you can get with its added black olives, olive oil and balsamic vinegar. It is rich in protective nutrients from both its olives and peppers. Colorful bell peppers provide high levels of vitamins and carotenoids with red peppers by far the richest in lycopene. Olives contain protective phytonutrients and healthy monounsaturated fats.

4 bell peppers (mixed colors)	Salt and pepper to taste
1 tbsp. olive oil	1 cup pitted black olives
1 tsp. balsamic vinegar	1 oz. fresh basil leaves

1 Preheat the broiler. Cut the peppers into thin slices and arrange them on a baking sheet. Spray some olive oil over the peppers or evenly distribute a tbsp. of olive oil over them. Broil for 10 minutes until the skins darken.

2 Put the peppers in a presentation dish and add balsamic vinegar, and salt and pepper. Garnish with olives and basil leaves.

Nutrition Information

Serving Size **1 Cup**   Servings **4**

Calories **108**	Potassium . . . . . . **351 mg**
Calories from fat **66**	Total Carbohydrates . . . **11 g**
Total Fat . . . . **7 g**	Dietary Fiber . . . . **5 g**
Cholesterol . . . . **0 mg**	Sugars . . . . **5 g**
Sodium . . . . **253 mg**	Protein . . . . **2 g**

Vitamin A . . . . **24 %**	Vitamin B6. . . . . . . **23 %**
Vitamin C . . . . . . **252 %**	Folic Acid. . . . . **6 %**
Calcium . . . . **6 %**	Pantothenic Acid . . . . **2 %**
Iron . . . . **11 %**	Phosphorus. . . . . **4 %**
Vitamin E. . . . . **9 %**	Magnesium. . . . . **6 %**
Vitamin K . . . . **57 %**	Zinc . . . . **2 %**
Vitamin B1 . . . . **7 %**	Copper . . . . **12 %**
Vitamin B2 . . . . **3 %**	Manganese . . . . **16 %**
Niacin . . . . **5 %**	

OTHER BENEFICIAL NUTRIENTS (PER SERVING)

Choline. . . . . **15 mg**
Beta-Carotene. . . . . **689 mcg**
Alpha-Carotene . . . . **39 mcg**
Lutein & Zeaxanthin. . . . . **1,205 mcg**

BELL PEPPER TARTAR
WITH POPPY SEEDS

4 CUPS • PREPARATION: 10 MINUTES • COOKING: 0 MINUTES • EASY

This is another quick and simple dish to prepare. It requires no cooking at all and it is packed with nutrition. Its combination of ingredients makes it a real crowd pleaser and it is great as a light appetizer or snack, but what I really love is how easy it is to prepare when I am short on time.

1 each red, yellow, orange bell peppers	1 tbsp. yogurt
½ medium red onion	1 tbsp. olive oil
2 tsp. agave or honey	Salt and pepper to taste
2 tsp. poppy seeds	Arugula or spinach for garnish

1 Wash and peel the peppers, cutting them into small, little squares; peel and chop the onion.

2 In a large bowl, mix the peppers, onion, agave, poppy seeds, yogurt, olive oil, salt and pepper. Serve in small bowls with some mixed greens for decoration.

Nutrition Information

Serving Size **1 Cup**   Servings **4**

Calories	**83**	Potassium	**233 mg**
Calories from fat	**40**	Total Carbohydrates	**10 g**
Total Fat	**4 g**	Dietary Fiber	**2 g**
Cholesterol	**1 mg**	Sugars	**5 g**
Sodium	**7 mg**	Protein	**2 g**

Vitamin A	**21 %**	Vitamin B6	**10 %**
Vitamin C	**67 %**	Folic Acid	**8 %**
Calcium	**4 %**	Pantothenic Acid	**2 %**
Iron	**3 %**	Phosphorus	**5 %**
Vitamin E	**5 %**	Magnesium	**4 %**
Vitamin K	**4 %**	Zinc	**2 %**
Vitamin B1	**4 %**	Selenium	**1 %**
Vitamin B2	**3 %**	Copper	**5 %**
Niacin	**4 %**	Manganese	**11 %**

OTHER BENEFICIAL NUTRIENTS (PER SERVING)

Choline	**6 mg**
Beta-Carotene	**555 mcg**
Alpha-Carotene	**6 mcg**
Lutein & Zeaxanthin	**16 mcg**

BELL PEPPER AND SNOW PEAS SHRIMP PAD THAI

6 - 7 CUPS • PREPARATION: 20 MINUTES • COOKING: 15 MINUTES • DIFFICULT

Everyone loves Pad Thai at the house. The flavors are so uniquely delicious and the resulting recipe is exceptionally nutritious. I was told that technically, I should not call this Pad Thai, because it does not contain rice noodles, but since we do not eat noodles, I will leave that to you to decide for yourself. We love it without noodles or rice and, regardless of how you eat it, I am sure you will fall in love with its classic exotic Asian flavors.

1 orange or red bell pepper, sliced

1 tbsp. dark sesame oil

1½ lbs. large shrimp, peeled

1½ lbs. sugar snap peas

1 tbsp. ginger, minced

½ cup roasted peanuts

For the Pad Thai sauce:

2 cloves garlic, minced

2 tbsp. peanut butter

1 tbsp. agave nectar or honey

1 tbsp. dark sesame oil

3 tbsp. low-sodium soy sauce

1 tbsp. ginger, minced (or 1 tsp. ground)

1 tsp. Sriracha (or red hot chili pepper flakes)

1 In a wok over medium to high heat, add 1 tbsp. of the sesame oil. Add the shrimp and cook for about 5 minutes until they turn pink. Remove the shrimp. Reserve on the side on a plate.

2 In the same wok over medium heat, combine the snow peas and pepper with the minced ginger. Cook for about 5 minutes.

3 During this time, make the sauce in a mini blender (or mix well in a bowl) adding the garlic, peanut butter, agave, sesame oil, low-sodium soy sauce, ginger, and Sriracha or red hot chili pepper. Mix very well until thick.

4   Put shrimp, vegetables and sauce in the wok. Cook together for 3 minutes. Serve with the roasted peanuts.

Nutrition Information

Serving Size 1 Cup   **Servings 6**

Calories	324	Potassium	598 mg
Calories from fat	110	Total Carbohydrates	29 g
Total Fat	12 g	Dietary Fiber	8 g
Cholesterol	143 mg	Sugars	14 g
Sodium	938 mg	Protein	27 g

Vitamin A	34 %	Vitamin B6	38 %
Vitamin C	119 %	Folic Acid	35 %
Calcium	11 %	Vitamin B12	21 %
Iron	19 %	Pantothenic Acid	7 %
Vitamin D3	1 %	Phosphorus	49 %
Vitamin E	26 %	Magnesium	27 %
Vitamin K	38 %	Zinc	28 %
Vitamin B1	25 %	Selenium	53 %
Vitamin B2	13 %	Copper	33 %
Niacin	36 %	Manganese	41 %

OTHER BENEFICIAL NUTRIENTS (PER SERVING)

Choline	180 mg
Beta-Carotene	995 mcg
Alpha-Carotene	28 mcg
Lutein & Zeaxanthin	2,916 mcg

LINDSEY'S STUFFED POBLANOS WITH QUINOA AND CHICKEN

6 – 8 SERVINGS • PREPARATION: 30 MINUTES • COOKING: 30 MINUTES • DIFFICULT

This recipe is a pleasant surprise. It is a bit time-consuming, particularly the first time through, but it is well worth the investment of time. Lindsey, our wonderful photographer for this book, gave me the inspiration for this delicious Southwest recipe. Poblano peppers are low in calories and fat and are rich in fiber and phytonutrients. I would divide each Poblano pepper between at least two people, since the poblano peppers we use are large and generously filled with chicken, tomatoes and tasty, protective herbs and spices. Quinoa makes a wonderful nutritious addition, since it is a complete protein and not a grain, being closely related to beets and spinach.

½ cup quinoa	1 lb. ground chicken	1 tsp. oregano
1 cup water	1 can (14.5 oz.) tomatoes, diced	8 oz. queso fresco, crumbled
4 poblano peppers	1 jalapeño, sliced	Salt and pepper to taste
½ medium red onion, chopped	1 tsp. cinnamon	¼ cup fresh cilantro, chopped
2 garlic cloves, minced	1 tsp. cumin	1 lime

1 Cook the quinoa according to the box; usually ½ cup quinoa to 1 cup water. Bring to a boil and reduce the heat to low. Cover and simmer for 15 minutes. Reserve.

2 Preheat the broiler and line a large-rimmed baking sheet with tin foil. Set the poblanos on the baking tray under the broiler for 4 minutes on each side. They come out quite dark.

3 Cut the hat off the poblanos. Remove the seeds. Be gentle.

4 In a skillet on medium heat, add a little olive oil and sauté the onion and garlic along with the ground chicken for approximately 5 to 7 minutes until almost cooked through.

5 Add the tomatoes, half of the sliced jalapeño, if you like it hot (otherwise just serve it on the side), cinnamon, cumin, oregano, queso fresco, salt and pepper, and cilantro. Cook everything together for 5 minutes.

6 Fill the poblanos with the stuffing. Serve with lime and a slice of jalapeño. We prefer to cut the peppers in half to double the servings.

Nutrition Information

Serving Size ½ **Large Poblano**   Servings **8**

Calories **239**	Potassium . . . . . . **592 mg**
Calories from fat . . . **120**	Total Carbohydrates . . . **13 g**
Total Fat . . . . **13 g**	Dietary Fiber . . . . **5 g**
Cholesterol . . . . . . **68 mg**	Sugars . . . . **3 g**
Sodium . . . . **252 mg**	Protein . . . . **18 g**

Vitamin A . . . . **15 %**	Vitamin B6. . . . . . . **28 %**
Vitamin C . . . . **95 %**	Folic Acid. . . . . **9 %**
Calcium . . . . **19 %**	Vitamin B12 . . . . . . **13 %**
Iron . . . . **9 %**	Pantothenic Acid . . . . **9 %**
Vitamin D3. . . . . . . **8 %**	Phosphorus . . . . **28 %**
Vitamin E. . . . . **6 %**	Magnesium. . . . . . . **13 %**
Vitamin K . . . . **23 %**	Zinc . . . . **14 %**
Vitamin B1 . . . . **11 %**	Selenium . . . . **18 %**
Vitamin B2. . . . . . . **15 %**	Copper. . . . . **9 %**
Niacin . . . . **19 %**	Manganese . . . . **19 %**

OTHER BENEFICIAL NUTRIENTS (PER SERVING)

Choline. . . . . **50 mg**
Beta-Carotene. . . . . **299 mcg**
Alpha-Carotene . . . . **38 mcg**
Lutein & Zeaxanthin. . . . . **347 mcg**
Lycopene. . . . . **611 mcg**

RED BELL PEPPER
"NUTTY HUMMUS"

2 CUPS • PREPARATION AND COOKING: 15 MINUTES (PLUS 2 HOURS) • EASY

Hummus is a dip or spread from the Middle East that has been traditionally made from mashed chickpeas (garbanzo beans). Hummus is still one of Andrew's favorite treats, but we wanted to have a lower-carb option as well. One day, while experimenting with some cashews I had soaked overnight, we came up with this amazing recipe. It has become one of our favorite dips for veggies or as a spread or sauce. In fact, we use it in our Savoy Cabbage, Watercress Veggie Rolls (Recipe #11). Consuming nuts is a healthy addition to any diet and combined with red bell peppers it is both tasty and even more nutritious.

1 red pepper	1 tbsp. olive oil	¼ to ½ cup water
1½ cups raw, unsalted cashews, soaked (2 hours min.)	1 tbsp. Tahini (sesame seed butter)	Pinch each salt and Cayenne pepper
2 garlic cloves	1 tsp. white wine vinegar	

1 Slice the pepper and remove the seeds. Place it on an oven tray covered with tin foil and a little olive oil, and roast in the oven for 10 minutes or until skin darkens.

2 Soak cashews in water for at least 2 hours or overnight. Drain the cashews. Place the cashews in blender.

3 Add garlic, roasted pepper, remaining olive oil, tahini, white wine vinegar, water, salt, black pepper and cayenne (to taste) into the blender. Blend approximately 3 minutes or until smooth. Add more water if necessary to obtain a smooth paste. You may chill before serving.

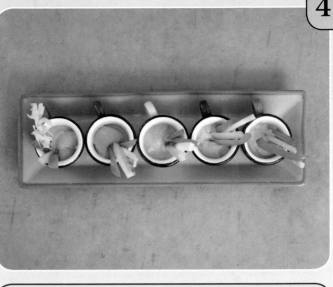

4 Julienne (thinly slice) a selection of vegetables for serving. I suggest cucumbers, carrots, orange pepper and celery.

5 Serve in individual bowls with the julienned vegetables nicely arranged around them.

Nutrition Information

Serving Size **1 tsp.**   Servings **32**

Calories	**36**	Potassium	**39 mg**
Calories from fat	**26**	Total Carbohydrates	**2 g**
Total Fat	**3 g**	Dietary Fiber	**1 g**
Cholesterol	**0 mg**	Sugars	**0 g**
Sodium	**1 mg**	Protein	**1 g**

Vitamin A	**2 %**	Folic Acid	**1 %**
Vitamin C	**8 %**	Pantothenic Acid	**1 %**
Iron	**2 %**	Phosphorus	**3 %**
Vitamin E	**1 %**	Magnesium	**4 %**
Vitamin K	**3 %**	Zinc	**2 %**
Vitamin B1	**1 %**	Selenium	**1 %**
Vitamin B2	**1 %**	Copper	**6 %**
Niacin	**1 %**	Manganese	**3 %**
Vitamin B6	**1 %**		

OTHER BENEFICIAL NUTRIENTS (PER SERVING)

Choline	**3 mg**
Beta-Carotene	**60 mcg**
Alpha-Carotene	**1 mcg**
Lutein & Zeaxanthin	**3 mcg**

TOMATO PROVENÇALE À LA MURIEL

6 SERVINGS • PREPARATION: 15 MINUTES • COOKING: 15 MINUTES • MEDIUM

This is a classic Mediterranean dish from the South of France that I have always enjoyed. It is extremely easy to make and I chose to add pistachios, since Andrew mentioned that they are among the healthiest nuts and he also adores their flavor. Many of us consider the tomato a vegetable and, despite an erroneous US Supreme Court decision declaring tomatoes a vegetable, they are technically a fruit – a very healthy, low calorie, nutrient-rich fruit.

3 large ripe tomatoes, cut in half horizontally

3 tbsp. olive oil

Salt and pepper to taste

2 cloves garlic, minced

1 tbsp. Herbs de Provence

1 oz. fresh basil, cut in thin strips

½ cup pistachios, crushed

1 Preheat the oven to 375°. Start cooking the tomatoes on the stove for 5 minutes over medium heat with 1 tbsp. olive oil, salt and pepper.

2 Mix together the minced garlic, Herbs de Provence, most of the basil (reserve some for serving) and the crushed pistachios.

3 Pour remaining olive oil on top of the tomatoes and then add the herb mixture on top of the tomatoes. Bake for 15 minutes. It's really good with a great steak.

Nutrition Information

Serving Size ½ **Tomato**   Servings **6**

Calories	**117**	Potassium	**340 mg**
Calories from fat	**84**	Total Carbohydrates	**7 g**
Total Fat	**9 g**	Dietary Fiber	**2 g**
Cholesterol	**0 mg**	Sugars	**3 g**
Sodium	**5 mg**	Protein	**3 g**

Vitamin A	**21 %**	Vitamin B6	**13 %**
Vitamin C	**24 %**	Folic Acid	**6 %**
Calcium	**3 %**	Pantothenic Acid	**2 %**
Iron	**5 %**	Phosphorus	**7 %**
Vitamin E	**7 %**	Magnesium	**6 %**
Vitamin K	**29 %**	Zinc	**3 %**
Vitamin B1	**8 %**	Selenium	**1 %**
Vitamin B2	**2 %**	Copper	**10 %**
Niacin	**4 %**	Manganese	**15 %**

OTHER BENEFICIAL NUTRIENTS (PER SERVING)

Choline	**7 mg**
Beta-Carotene	**591 mcg**
Alpha-Carotene	**92 mcg**
Lutein & Zeaxanthin	**539 mcg**
Lycopene	**2,341 mcg**

TOMATO MARINARA SAUCE

4 CUPS • PREPARATION: 15 MINUTES • COOKING: 20 MINUTES • MEDIUM

This simple sauce is a classic low-calorie staple of the healthy Mediterranean diet and Andrew loves it. I often find him eating it like a soup or using it as a dip or condiment with almost anything he eats. It can of course be used for pasta, but since we do not eat pasta, we use it as a nutritious, low-calorie alternative to catsup, mustard, mayonnaise or high-calorie sauces or dressings. It is rich in lycopene and perfect for use with our Kale Turkey Burgers (Recipe #3).

4 or 5 (2 lbs.) large, ripe tomatoes	3 garlic cloves, minced
1 can (14.5 oz) tomatoes, diced	1 oz. fresh basil
3 tbsp. olive oil	1 tsp. agave or honey
2 shallots, minced	Salt and pepper to taste

1 In a small saucepan, bring water to a boil. Plant a fork in each tomato and soak in the boiling water for 2 minutes.

2 Peel with a knife. The skin should come off effortlessly.

3 Cut the tomatoes in quarters and remove the seeds with a spoon.

4 In a large saucepan over medium heat, add the olive oil and sauté the garlic and shallots for one minute.

5 Combine the peeled and seeded tomatoes, the can of diced tomatoes, salt and pepper, and the agave. Cook for 15 minutes until the tomatoes are dark red.

6 Pour everything in the blender and mix for 1 to 2 minutes. Add the basil at the end. The basil is usually minced very finely.

Nutrition Information

Serving Size **1 tbsp.**   Servings **64**

Calories	**10**	Potassium	**49 mg**
Calories from fat	**6**	Total Carbohydrates	**1 g**
Total Fat	**1 g**	Dietary Fiber	**0 g**
Cholesterol	**0 mg**	Sugars	**1 g**
Sodium	**1 mg**	Protein	**0 g**

Vitamin A	**3 %**	Vitamin B6	**1 %**
Vitamin C	**4 %**	Folic Acid	**1 %**
Iron	**1 %**	Phosphorus	**1 %**
Vitamin E	**1 %**	Magnesium	**1 %**
Vitamin K	**4 %**	Copper	**1 %**
Vitamin B1	**1 %**	Manganese	**1 %**
Niacin	**1 %**		

OTHER BENEFICIAL NUTRIENTS (PER SERVING)

Choline	**2 mg**
Beta-Carotene	**82 mcg**
Alpha-Carotene	**14 mcg**
Lutein & Zeaxanthin	**48 mcg**
Lycopene	**543 mcg**

TURMERIC CURRY OF PINEAPPLE WITH CARROTS, COCONUT AND CINNAMON

10 CUPS • PREPARATION: 15 MINUTES • COOKING: 20 MINUTES • MEDIUM

This dish combines two of our favorites, since we love curry at the house and we also eat a great deal of enzyme-rich fruits, such as pineapple and papaya. You can't help but feel a healthy peace of mind when you look at all the beautiful healthy colors of the ingredients in this recipe and then consider the phytonutrient content of turmeric, cinnamon, ginger, garlic and onions. If we could all eat food like this every day, we would reap enormous healthy benefits.

1 tsp. coconut oil

1 medium red onion, chopped
(or 2 small shallots)

2 cloves garlic, minced

1 tbsp. ginger, minced

2 cups carrots, sliced

1 tsp. turmeric

1 lb. (3 cups) sugar snap peas

1 can (13.5 oz.) light coconut milk

3 cups pineapple, cubed

1 tsp. cinnamon

1 tsp. red chili pepper flakes

1 pinch of salt

1 Star Anise

1 In a large wok or skillet over medium heat, melt the coconut oil. Add the chopped onion, garlic, ginger, sliced carrots and turmeric. Sauté for 10 minutes or until carrots soften.

2 Add the sugar snap peas and sauté for 2 minutes Add the coconut milk and cook approximately 6 additional minutes until the sugar snap peas are bright green and tender. Add the salt.

3 Add the pineapple, cinnamon and chili flakes, salt and Star Anise. Cook for 3 more minutes. Serve in individual bowls.

Nutrition Information

Serving Size **1 Cup**   Servings **10**

Calories	161	Potassium	371 mg
Calories from fat	81	Total Carbohydrates	19 g
Total Fat	9 g	Dietary Fiber	4 g
Cholesterol	0 mg	Sugars	9 g
Sodium	26 mg	Protein	4 g

Vitamin A	89 %	Vitamin B6	11 %
Vitamin C	75 %	Folic Acid	13 %
Calcium	4 %	Pantothenic Acid	3 %
Iron	13 %	Phosphorus	11 %
Vitamin E	2 %	Magnesium	11 %
Vitamin K	19 %	Zinc	6 %
Vitamin B1	13 %	Selenium	2 %
Vitamin B2	6 %	Copper	12 %
Niacin	9 %	Manganese	54 %

OTHER BENEFICIAL NUTRIENTS (PER SERVING)

Choline	39 mg
Beta-Carotene	2,341 mcg
Alpha-Carotene	858 mcg
Lutein & Zeaxanthin	1,247 mcg

TURMERIC COCONUT CURRY OF SWEET POTATO WITH ENGLISH PEAS AND TOFU

9 - 10 CUPS • PREPARATION: 20 MINUTES • COOKING: 25 MINUTES • MEDIUM

For decades, Andrew has talked about the protective health benefits from turmeric (curry) and it has become one of our favorite spices at home. He has also mentioned that if you are going to eat a potato, then it would be good to avoid the white potatoes and the best and most nutritious choice is a "non-potato" - the sweet potato. At Andrew's request, I have often substituted minced chicken for the tofu.

2 large (1½ to 2 lbs.) sweet potatoes

1 medium red onion

1 tbsp. coconut or sesame oil

2 cloves garlic, diced

1 tsp. turmeric

1 bay leaf

1 cup cooked or smoked tofu

1 can (14.5 oz.) diced tomatoes

1 can (14 oz.) light coconut milk

1 cup English peas

Salt and pepper to taste

Red chili pepper flakes

1 Peel sweet potatoes and dice into little squares; chop onion.

2 In a wok or large skillet, melt coconut oil (reserving some for later) and sauté the onion, garlic, turmeric, bay leaf and sweet potatoes for 5 minutes over medium heat.

3 Cube tofu and sauté with the remaining coconut oil over medium heat. Reserve.

4 Add diced tomatoes and coconut milk. Cover and simmer over low heat for 15 minutes.

5 Add peas and cook for 5 additional minutes on low to medium heat until potatoes are tender. Add tofu, salt and pepper to taste.

6 Add red hot chili pepper flakes, if desired. Serve warm.

Nutrition Information

Serving Size **1 Cup**   Servings **10**

Calories	**118**	Potassium	**259 mg**
Calories from fat	**67**	Total Carbohydrates	**10 g**
Total Fat	**7 g**	Dietary Fiber	**2 g**
Cholesterol	**0 mg**	Sugars	**3 g**
Sodium	**22 mg**	Protein	**4 g**
Vitamin A	**76 %**	Vitamin B6	**7 %**
Vitamin C	**16 %**	Folic Acid	**6 %**
Calcium	**11 %**	Pantothenic Acid	**3 %**
Iron	**15 %**	Phosphorus	**8 %**
Vitamin E	**1 %**	Magnesium	**8 %**
Vitamin K	**6 %**	Zinc	**4 %**
Vitamin B1	**7 %**	Selenium	**4 %**
Vitamin B2	**4 %**	Copper	**9 %**
Niacin	**4 %**	Manganese	**25 %**

OTHER BENEFICIAL NUTRIENTS (PER SERVING)

Choline	**17 mg**
Beta-Carotene	**2,291 mcg**
Alpha-Carotene	**5 mcg**
Lutein & Zeaxanthin	**376 mcg**
Lycopene	**526 mcg**

INDEX

A Agave

Brussels Sprouts Sautéed with Sesame Seeds Asian Style 8
Andrew's Favorite Chopped Chicken and Cabbage Salad 10
Vietnamese Cabbage Salad. 12
Diced Asparagus, Avocado and Tomato Tartar 26
Asparagus, Salmon and Baby Corn Asian Sauté 28
Bell Pepper Tartar with Poppy Seeds 38
Bell Pepper and Snow Peas Shrimp Pad Thai 39
Tomato Marinara Sauce. 43

Almonds

Michelle's Kale and Brussels Sprouts Chopped Salad 4
Sautéed Brussels Sprouts with Almonds 7
Cauliflower and Tomato Casserole with Almonds and Parmesan. 21
Zucchini Casserole with Almonds and Parmesan Cheese 35

Almond (meal)

Andrew's Mashed Cauliflower 20
Zucchini Casserole with Almonds and Parmesan Cheese 35

Apple (juice)

Savory Salad with Red Cabbage and Pineapple. 13

Apricots (dried)

Rainbow Swiss Chard Sautéed with Pine Nuts and Dried Apricots 32

Arugula

Bell Pepper Tartar with Poppy Seeds 38

Asparagus

Diced Asparagus, Avocado and Tomato Tartar 26
Asparagus Bundles in Prosciutto with Parmesan 27
Asparagus, Salmon and Baby Corn Asian Sauté 28
Sautéed Asparagus to "Bragg" About 29
Very Green Asparagus Risotto. 30

Avocado

Andrew's Favorite Chopped Chicken and Cabbage Salad 10
Savoy Cabbage, Watercress Veggie Rolls 11
Diced Asparagus, Avocado and Tomato Tartar 26

B Baby Corn

Asparagus, Salmon and Baby Corn Asian Sauté 28

Basil

Eggplant Parmigiana with Kale 6

Very Green Asparagus Risotto 30
Roasted Bell Peppers with Olives 37
Tomato Provençale à la Muriél 42
Tomato Marinara Sauce 43

Bay Leaf
Turmeric Curry of Sweet Potato with English Peas and Tofu 45

Beans (black)
Andrew's Favorite Chopped Chicken and Cabbage Salad 10

Beans (green)
Broccolini and Green Bean Lettuce Cups 17
Collard Greens and Green Beans à l'Orange 23
Wasabi Smoked Salmon Green Bean Rolls 25

Bragg Liquid Aminos
Sautéed Asparagus to "Bragg" About 29

Broccoli
Broccoli and Shrimp Sautéed with Chili Flakes and Shredded Coconut 14
Broccoli "Soufflé" 15
Andrew's Favorite Grilled Broccoli 16

Broccolini
Broccolini and Green Bean Lettuce Cups 17

Broth (chicken)
Stuffed Bell Peppers with Millet, Mushrooms and Turmeric 36

Broth (vegetable)
Andrew's Mashed Cauliflower 20
Very Green Asparagus Risotto 30
Swiss Chard Casserole with Quinoa and Tomatoes 34
Stuffed Bell Peppers with Millet, Mushrooms and Turmeric 36

Brussels Sprouts
Michelle's Kale and Brussels Sprouts Chopped Salad 4
Sautéed Brussels Sprouts with Almonds 7
Brussels Sprouts Sautéed with Sesame Seeds Asian Style 8
Brussels Sprout *Gratin* 9

Butter
Brussels Sprout *Gratin* 9
Broccoli "Soufflé" 15
Cauliflower Casserole de ma Grand-mère 19
Andrew's Mashed Cauliflower 20

C Cabbage
Andrew's Favorite Chopped Chicken and Cabbage Salad 10

Cabbage (Chinese)
Savoy Cabbage, Watercress Veggie Rolls 11
Vietnamese Cabbage Salad 12

Cabbage (red)
    Incredible Kale, Red Cabbage and Pomegranate Salad 1
    Kale, Red Cabbage and Roasted Eggplant 5
    Savory Salad with Red Cabbage and Pineapple 13

Carrots
    Vietnamese Cabbage Salad 12
    Turmeric Curry of Pineapple with Carrots, Coconut and Cinnamon 44

Cashews
    Vietnamese Cabbage Salad 12
    Wasabi-Watercress *Nutty Hummus* 24
    Red Bell Pepper *Nutty Hummus* 41

Cauliflower
    Andrew's Favorite Grilled Cauliflower 18
    Cauliflower Casserole de ma Grand-mère 19
    Andrew's Mashed Cauliflower 20
    Cauliflower and Tomato Casserole with Almonds and Parmesan 21

Chard (Rainbow Swiss)
    Swiss Chard with Shiitake Mushrooms 31
    Rainbow Swiss Chard Sautéed with Pine Nuts and Dried Apricots 32
    Swiss Chard Egg-white Frittata de Provence with Feta Cheese 33
    Swiss Chard Casserole with Quinoa and Tomatoes 34

Cheese (feta)
    Swiss Chard Egg-white Frittata de Provence with Feta Cheese 33

Cheese (goat)
    Broccolini and Green Bean Lettuce Cups 17

Cheese (mozzarella)
    Eggplant Parmigiana with Kale 6
    Swiss Chard Casserole with Quinoa and Tomatoes 34

Cheese (Parmesan)
    Incredible Kale, Red Cabbage and Pomegranate Salad 1
    Michelle's Kale and Brussels Sprouts Chopped Salad 4
    Eggplant Parmigiana with Kale 6
    Brussels Sprout *Gratin* 9
    Cauliflower and Tomato Casserole with Almonds and Parmesan 21
    Egg-white Frittata with Collard Greens, Zucchini & Turmeric 22
    Asparagus Bundles in Prosciutto with Parmesan 27
    Very Green Asparagus Risotto 30
    Zucchini Casserole with Almonds and Parmesan Cheese .35

Cheese (queso fresco)
    Lindsey's Stuffed Poblanos with Quinoa and Chicken 40

Cheese (Ricotta)
    Brussels Sprout *Gratin* 9

Cheese (Swiss)
    Broccoli "Soufflé"...............................15
    Cauliflower Casserole de ma Grand-mère 19
Chicken (Breast)
    Andrew's Favorite Chopped Chicken and Cabbage Salad.............10
Chicken (ground)
    Lindsey's Stuffed Poblanos with Quinoa and Chicken...............40
Chipotle Seasoning
    Andrew's Favorite Chopped Chicken and Cabbage Salad.............10
Chives
    Savory Salad with Red Cabbage and Pineapple...............13
    Cauliflower and Tomato Casserole with Almonds and Parmesan...............21
Cilantro
    Michelle's Kale and Brussels Sprouts Chopped Salad 4
    Andrew's Favorite Chopped Chicken and Cabbage Salad...............10
    Lindsey's Stuffed Poblanos with Quinoa and Chicken...............40
Cinnamon
    Lindsey's Stuffed Poblanos with Quinoa and Chicken...............40
    Turmeric Curry of Pineapple with Carrots, Coconut and Cinnamon 44
Coconut
    Broccoli and Shrimp Sautéed with Chili Flakes and Shredded Coconut...............14
Collard Greens
    Egg-white Frittata with Collard Greens, Zucchini & Turmeric...............22
    Collard Greens and Green Beans à l'Orange...............23
Corn
    Andrew's Favorite Chopped Chicken and Cabbage Salad...............10
Cornstarch
    Broccoli "Soufflé"...............15
    Asparagus, Salmon and Baby Corn Asian Sauté 28
Crackers
    Wasabi-Watercress "Nutty Hummus"...............24
Cranberries (dried)
    Rainbow Swiss Chard Sautéed with Pine Nuts and Dried Apricots...............32
Cumin
    Kale Turkey Burgers 3
    Savory Salad with Red Cabbage and Pineapple...............13
    Stuffed Bell Peppers with Millet, Mushrooms and Turmeric...............36
    Lindsey's Stuffed Poblanos with Quinoa and Chicken...............40

E Eggs
    Kale Turkey Burgers 3
    Brussels Sprout Gratin 9
    Broccoli "Soufflé"...............15

Zucchini Casserole with Almonds and Parmesan Cheese 35

Eggs (whites)

    Eggplant Parmigiana with Kale 6

    Egg-white Frittata with Collard Greens, Zucchini & Turmeric 22

    Swiss Chard Egg-white Frittata de Provence with Feta Cheese 33

Eggplant

    Kale, Red Cabbage and Roasted Eggplant 5

    Eggplant Parmigiana with Kale 6

F Fish Sauce

    Vietnamese Cabbage Salad. 12

    Bell Pepper and Snow Peas Shrimp Pad Thai 39

Flour (Garbanzo)

    Eggplant Parmigiana with Kale 6

    Broccoli "Soufflé" 15

    Cauliflower Casserole de ma Grand-mère 19

G Ginger

    Brussels Sprouts Sautéed with Sesame Seeds Asian Style 8

    Vietnamese Cabbage Salad. 12

    Broccoli and Shrimp Sautéed with Chili Flakes and Shredded Coconut. 14

    Asparagus, Salmon and Baby Corn Asian Sauté 28

    Bell Pepper and Snow Peas Shrimp Pad Thai 39

    Turmeric Curry of Pineapple with Carrots, Coconut and Cinnamon 44

H Herbs de Provence

    Tomato Provençale à la Muriél. 42

Herbs de Provence (with Lavender)

    Swiss Chard Egg-white Frittata de Provence with Feta Cheese 33

Honey

    Brussels Sprouts Sautéed with Sesame Seeds Asian Style 8

    Vietnamese Cabbage Salad. 12

    Diced Asparagus, Avocado and Tomato Tartar 26

    Bell Pepper Tartar with Poppy Seeds 38

    Bell Pepper and Snow Peas Shrimp Pad Thai 39

    Tomato Marinara Sauce. 43

J Jalapeño

    Lindsey's Stuffed Poblanos with Quinoa and Chicken. 40

K Kale

    Incredible Kale, Red Cabbage and Pomegranate Salad 1

    Kale with Roasted Butternut Squash and Marjoram 2

Kale Turkey Burgers 3
Michelle's Kale and Brussels Sprouts Chopped Salad 4
Kale, Red Cabbage and Roasted Eggplant 5
Eggplant Parmigiana with Kale 6

L Lemon (organic)
Brussels Sprout *Gratin* 9
Lemon (juice)
Incredible Kale, Red Cabbage and Pomegranate Salad 1
Michelle's Kale and Brussels Sprouts Chopped Salad 4
Andrew's Favorite Grilled Cauliflower 18
Diced Asparagus, Avocado and Tomato Tartar 26
Red Bell Pepper "*Nutty Hummus*" 41
Rainbow Swiss Chard Sautéed with Pine Nuts and Dried Apricots 32
Lettuce (Bibb)
Broccolini and Green Bean Lettuce Cups 17
Lime
Lindsey's Stuffed Poblanos with Quinoa and Chicken 40
Lime (juice)
Kale, Red Cabbage and Roasted Eggplant 5
Andrew's Favorite Chopped Chicken and Cabbage Salad 10
Vietnamese Cabbage Salad 12
Broccoli and Shrimp Sautéed with Chili Flakes and Shredded Coconut 14

M Marinara Sauce
Kale Turkey Burgers 3
Eggplant Parmigiana with Kale 6
Marjoram
Kale with Roasted Butternut Squash and Marjoram 2
Milk (heavy cream)
Swiss Chard with Shiitake Mushrooms 31
Milk (light coconut)
Turmeric Curry of Pineapple with Carrots, Coconut and Cinnamon 44
Turmeric Curry of Sweet Potato with English Peas and Tofu 45
Milk (skim)
Broccoli "Soufflé" 15
Cauliflower Casserole de ma Grand-mère 19
Zucchini Casserole with Almonds and Parmesan Cheese 35
Millet
Stuffed Bell Peppers with Millet, Mushrooms and Turmeric 36
Mint
Savoy Cabbage, Watercress Veggie Rolls 11
Vietnamese Cabbage Salad 12

Wasabi–Watercress "*Nutty Hummus*"................................24
Diced Asparagus, Avocado and Tomato Tartar...............26
Mushrooms
Stuffed Bell Peppers with Millet, Mushrooms and Turmeric..........36
Mushrooms (Shiitake)
Swiss Chard with Shiitake Mushrooms....................31
Mustard (Dijon)
Michelle's Kale and Brussels Sprouts Chopped Salad..........4
Broccolini and Green Bean Lettuce Cups.................17

N Nutmeg
Broccoli "Soufflé"..................................15
Cauliflower Casserole de ma Grand-mère...............19
Zucchini Casserole with Almonds and Parmesan Cheese......35
Nuts (peanuts)
Bell Pepper and Snow Peas Shrimp Pad Thai.............39
Nuts (pine)
Incredible Kale, Red Cabbage and Pomegranate Salad......1
Very Green Asparagus Risotto........................30
Rainbow Swiss Chard Sautéed with Pine Nuts and Dried Apricots....32
Stuffed Bell Peppers with Millet, Mushrooms and Turmeric.....36
Nuts (pistachios)
Tomato Provençale à la Muriél.......................42

O Olives (black)
Roasted Bell Peppers with Olives....................37
Onion (green)
Andrew's Favorite Chopped Chicken and Cabbage Salad......10
Onion (red)
Kale with Roasted Butternut Squash and Marjoram........2
Kale Turkey Burgers................................3
Brussels Sprout *Gratin*............................9
Egg-white Frittata with Collard Greens, Zucchini & Turmeric....22
Very Green Asparagus Risotto........................30
Rainbow Swiss Chard Sautéed with Pine Nuts and Dried Apricots....32
Swiss Chard Egg-white Frittata de Provence with Feta Cheese....33
Swiss Chard Casserole with Quinoa and Tomatoes........34
Stuffed Bell Peppers with Millet, Mushrooms and Turmeric.....36
Bell Pepper Tartar with Poppy Seeds..................38
Lindsey's Stuffed Poblanos with Quinoa and Chicken......40
Turmeric Curry of Pineapple with Carrots, Coconut and Cinnamon....44
Turmeric Curry of Sweet Potato with English Peas and Tofu....45

Orange (juice)
    Collard Greens and Green Beans à l'Orange 23
Orange (zest)
    Collard Greens and Green Beans à l'Orange 23
Oregano
    Lindsey's Stuffed Poblanos with Quinoa and Chicken 40

P

Pancetta
    Asparagus Bundles in Prosciutto with Parmesan 27
Paprika
    Kale Turkey Burgers 3
    Cauliflower and Tomato Casserole with Almonds and Parmesan 21
Parsley
    Broccolini and Green Bean Lettuce Cups 17
    Swiss Chard with Shiitake Mushrooms 31
    Stuffed Bell Peppers with Millet, Mushrooms and Turmeric 36
Peanut Butter
    Bell Pepper and Snow Peas Shrimp Pad Thai 39
Peas (English)
    Turmeric Curry of Sweet Potato with English Peas and Tofu 45
Peas (snow)
    Bell Pepper and Snow Peas Shrimp Pad Thai 39
Peas (sugar snap)
    Turmeric Curry of Pineapple with Carrots, Coconut and Cinnamon 44
Pepper (orange, red, yellow)
    Savoy Cabbage, Watercress Veggie Rolls 11
    Collard Greens and Green Beans à l'Orange 23
    Bell Pepper and Snow Peas Shrimp Pad Thai 39
    Stuffed Bell Peppers with Millet, Mushrooms and Turmeric 36
    Roasted Bell Peppers with Olives 37
    Bell Pepper Tartar with Poppy Seeds 38
    Red Bell Pepper *Nutty Hummus* 41
Pineapple
    Savory Salad with Red Cabbage and Pineapple 13
    Turmeric Curry of Pineapple with Carrots, Coconut and Cinnamon 44
Pita Bread
    Wasabi-Watercress *"Nutty Hummus"* 24
Poblanos
    Lindsey's Stuffed Poblanos with Quinoa and Chicken 40
Pomegranate (seeds)
    Incredible Kale, Red Cabbage and Pomegranate Salad 1
Poppy (seeds)
    Bell Pepper Tartar with Poppy Seeds 38

Potatoes (sweet)
    Turmeric Curry of Sweet Potato with English Peas and Tofu 45
Potatoes (Yams)
    Turmeric Curry of Sweet Potato with English Peas and Tofu 45
Prosciutto
    Asparagus Bundles in Prosciutto with Parmesan 27
Pumpkin (seeds)
    Kale with Roasted Butternut Squash and Marjoram 2

Q Quinoa
    Swiss Chard Casserole with Quinoa and Tomatoes 34
    Lindsey's Stuffed Poblanos with Quinoa and Chicken 40

R Radish
    Vietnamese Cabbage Salad 12
Raisins
    Kale, Red Cabbage and Roasted Eggplant 5
Rice (Arborio)
    Very Green Asparagus Risotto 30
Rice (brown)
    Very Green Asparagus Risotto 30
Rice Paper
    Wasabi Smoked Salmon Green Bean Rolls 25
Rosemary
    Andrew's Mashed Cauliflower 20
    Collard Greens and Green Beans à l'Orange 23
Salmon (smoked)
    Wasabi Smoked Salmon Green Bean Rolls 25
    Asparagus, Salmon and Baby Corn Asian Sauté 28

S Scallions
    Andrew's Favorite Chopped Chicken and Cabbage Salad 10
Sesame Seeds
    Brussels Sprouts Sautéed with Sesame Seeds Asian Style 8
    Kale, Red Cabbage and Roasted Eggplant 5
Shallots
    Kale Turkey Burgers 3
    Sautéed Brussels Sprouts with Almonds 7
    Brussels Sprout *Gratin* 9
    Broccolini and Green Bean Lettuce Cups 17
    Collard Greens and Green Beans à l'Orange 23
    Swiss Chard with Shiitake Mushrooms 31
    Tomato Marinara Sauce 43

Shrimp
    Broccoli and Shrimp Sautéed with Chili Flakes and Shredded Coconut 14
    Bell Pepper and Snow Peas Shrimp Pad Thai 39
Sriracha
    Kale, Red Cabbage and Roasted Eggplant 5
    Diced Asparagus, Avocado and Tomato Tartar 26
    Bell Pepper and Snow Peas Shrimp Pad Thai 39
Soy Sauce
    Brussels Sprouts Sautéed with Sesame Seeds Asian Style 8
    Vietnamese Cabbage Salad 12
    Asparagus, Salmon and Baby Corn Asian Sauté 28
    Sautéed Asparagus to "Bragg" About 29
    Bell Pepper and Snow Peas Shrimp Pad Thai 39
Spinach
    Bell Pepper Tartar with Poppy Seeds 38
Sprouts (daikon)
    Wasabi Smoked Salmon Green Bean Rolls 25
Squash (butternut)
    Kale with Roasted Butternut Squash and Marjoram 2
Star Anise
    Turmeric Curry of Pineapple with Carrots, Coconut and Cinnamon 44

T Tahini
    Wasabi-Watercress *Nutty Hummus* 24
    Red Bell Pepper *Nutty Hummus* 41
Tarragon
    Diced Asparagus, Avocado and Tomato Tartar 26
Thyme
    Sautéed Brussels Sprouts with Almonds 7
    Brussels Sprout *Gratin* 9
Tobasco
    Diced Asparagus, Avocado and Tomato Tartar 26
Tofu
    Vietnamese Cabbage Salad 12
    Egg-white Frittata with Collard Greens, Zucchini & Turmeric 22
    Turmeric Curry of Sweet Potato with English Peas and Tofu 45
Tomato
    Tomato Provençale à la Muriél 42
    Tomato Marinara Sauce 43
Tomato (cherry)
    Andrew's Favorite Chopped Chicken and Cabbage Salad 10
    Cauliflower and Tomato Casserole with Almonds and Parmesan 21
    Diced Asparagus, Avocado and Tomato Tartar 26

Swiss Chard Egg-white Frittata de Provence with Feta Cheese 33

Tomato (diced, canned)
    Cauliflower and Tomato Casserole with Almonds and Parmesan. 21
    Swiss Chard Casserole with Quinoa and Tomatoes 34
    Tomato Marinara Sauce. 43
    Lindsey's Stuffed Poblanos with Quinoa and Chicken. 40
    Turmeric Curry of Sweet Potato with English Peas and Tofu 45

Turkey (ground)
    Kale Turkey Burgers 3

Turmeric
    Egg-white Frittata with Collard Greens, Zucchini & Turmeric. 22
    Stuffed Bell Peppers with Millet, Mushrooms and Turmeric 36
    Turmeric Curry of Pineapple with Carrots, Coconut and Cinnamon 44
    Turmeric Curry of Sweet Potato with English Peas and Tofu 45

V Vinegar (apple cider)
    Savory Salad with Red Cabbage and Pineapple 13

Vinegar (balsamic)
    Broccolini and Green Bean Lettuce Cups. 17
    Collard Greens and Green Beans à l'Orange. 23
    Roasted Bell Peppers with Olives 37

Vinegar (white wine)
    Red Bell Pepper "*Nutty Hummus*" 41

W Wasabi
    Wasabi-Watercress "*Nutty Hummus*". 24

Watercress
    Kale Turkey Burgers 3
    Savoy Cabbage, Watercress Veggie Rolls 11
    Wasabi-Watercress "*Nutty Hummus*". 24

Wine (Mirin – Japanese rice)
    Asparagus, Salmon and Baby Corn Asian Sauté 28

Wine (white)
    Very Green Asparagus Risotto. 30

Y Yogurt
    Cauliflower and Tomato Casserole with Almonds and Parmesan. 21
    Bell Pepper Tartar with Poppy Seeds 38

Z Zucchini
    Egg-white Frittata with Collard Greens, Zucchini & Turmeric. 22
    Zucchini Casserole with Almonds and Parmesan Cheese 35